P9-BXZ-420

OUTSIDER

FICTION

Our Freedom to Read

• • • • • • • • • •

Coming-of-Age Fiction

Outsider Fiction

Classic Books

Science Fiction and Fantasy

OUTSIDER
FICTION

STEVEN OTFINOSKI

CHELSEA HOUSE
PUBLISHERS
An imprint of Infobase Publishing

Chelsea House
An imprint of Infobase Publishing
132 West 31st Street
New York, NY 10001

Library of Congress Cataloging-in-Publication Data
Otfinoski, Steven.
Our freedom to read / Steven Otfinoski.
v. cm.
Includes bibliographical references and indexes.
Contents: [1] Classic books — [2] Coming-of-age fiction —
[3] Outsider fiction — [4] Science fiction and fantasy.
ISBN 978-1-60413-029-4 (v. 1 : acid-free paper) — ISBN 978-1-60413-030-0
(v. 2 : acid-free paper) — ISBN 978-1-60413-031-7 (v. 3 : acid-free paper) —
ISBN 978-1-60413-032-4 (v. 4 : acid-free paper)
1. Prohibited books—Bibliography—Juvenile literature. 2. Challenged books—Bibliography—
Juvenile literature. 3. Expurgated books—Bibliography—Juvenile literature. 4. Prohibited
books—United States—Bibliography—Juvenile literature. 5. Challenged books—United States—
Bibliography—Juvenile literature. 6. Expurgated books—United States—Bibliography—Juvenile
literature. 7. Children's stories—Censorship—United States—Case studies—Juvenile literature.
8. Young adult fiction—Censorship—United States—Case studies—Juvenile literature.
9. Children's stories—Bio-bibliography—Juvenile literature. 10. Young adult fiction—
Bio-bibliography—Juvenile literature. I. Title.
Z1019.O84 2009
098'.1—dc22
2008032030

Text design by Erika K. Arroyo
Cover design by Ben Peterson

Printed in the United States of America

Bang KT 10 9 8 7 6 5 4 3 2 1

This book is printed on acid-free paper.

Contents

Introduction

EVERYONE HAS FELT LIKE AN OUTSIDER AT SOME TIME IN HIS OR HER life. It might come about from the experience of moving to a new city or town. Or it could be more inclusive—like being gay or disabled in a seemingly "normal" world. The first experience is temporary and will change with time, while in the other cases a person could remain an outsider for a lifetime.

Many people feel like outsiders during the awkward time of adolescence. Middle and high school are often testing grounds for conformity and acceptance by one's peers. Those who fail the test to "fit in" athletically, academically, or socially feel the pain and anguish of being shunned and made fun of. In actuality, the "in" crowd at school is often small and selective, leaving a majority of outsiders who may band together and form their own social groups. Nevertheless, those who are the most "different," by birth or choice, often pay a high price. Nothing can hurt more in these formative years than being rejected by your peers.

The world of the outsider rarely appeared in young-adult fiction before the mid-1960s. Teen novels and stories generally were about winners, not losers. Often the world these fictional characters inhabited was one that was far removed from the reality of young readers. That fictional world was safe, self-contained, and free of larger conflicts. In contrast, the real world, especially by the 1960s, was turbulent, confusing, and often unforgiving. Then there appeared in 1966 a novel, appropriately named *The Outsiders*, written by a young girl who saw herself as an outsider. The novel dealt with the haves and the have-nots in the youth culture of a small, western city. It was about gangs, sex, violence, fighting, and, ultimately, death. And young-adult fiction was never the same again.

Since then, young-adult authors have plumbed the depths of alienated youth. The wide range of outsider fiction is well represented in the 20 books considered in this collection. They include the overweight (*Blubber, Daughters of Eve*); gays, both male (*The Drowning of Stephan Jones, The Perks of Being a Wallflower*) and female (*Annie on My Mind*); drug addicts (*Go Ask Alice*); African Americans (*Fallen Angels, The Bluest Eye, Nappy Hair*); biracial and multiracial young people (*America, Whale Talk*); nerds and losers (*The Goats, The Perks of Being a Wallflower*); incarcerated youths (*The Buffalo Tree*); the sexually abused (*The Bluest Eye, America*); and even the elderly (*The Pigman*).

While most of these outsider novels take place in contemporary settings, three of them look back at America's past and show us that our country has been prejudiced for a long time against those who are different. *Fools Crow* deals with the disenfranchisement of the American Indian in the late 1800s. *Summer of My German Soldier* is about hatred toward our enemies in World War II America and also shows that prejudice against Jews was not confined to Nazi Germany. *Baseball Saved Us* depicts a shameful chapter of American history in the same time period, when thousands of loyal Japanese Americans were taken from their homes and sent to live in special detention camps simply because the homeland of their ancestors—Japan—was our wartime enemy. Interestingly, the author of each of these books had a personal stake in these stories—James Welch was Native American, Bette Greene is Jewish, and Ken Mochizuki is the son of Japanese Americans who lived in a World War II internment camp in Idaho.

Robert Cormier's *The Chocolate War* and *I Am the Cheese* take the idea of the outsider to new dramatic heights. Jerry Renault, the young protagonist in *The Chocolate War*, could conform, if he chose, to the rigid Catholic school he attends. But he chooses not to do so and pays a dear price for his stubborn individualism. Adam Farmer and his parents in *I Am the Cheese* are the helpless victims of a dark government conspiracy from which there is no escape; he may be the ultimate young outsider.

While Cormier's two novels end grimly with little hope, many of these other books are more optimistic. Some of the fictional outsiders struggle against adversity and succeed in finding their own worth and self-respect. The Japanese-American boy in *Baseball Saved Us* finds acceptance and a new sense of identity through sports, as does the motley swim team in *Whale Talk*. The two summer-camp outcasts in *The Goats* learn new survival skills and gain self-confidence in their struggle to escape from the camp and its deadening conformity. The little African-American girl in *Nappy Hair* learns to take pride in her appearance and to see it as an important symbol of her African heritage. Even the downtrodden Native Americans in *Fools Crow* learn to adapt to the white man's ways while still retaining their culture and unique identity.

Yet there is one battle that these books and their authors continue to fight—the battle of censorship. The honesty and fierceness the authors poured into their books have made them outsiders at times in school classrooms and libraries. Of the 20 books considered here, 12 made the American Library Association's "100 Most Frequently Challenged Books of 1990–2000." Three of them are in the ALA's "10 Most Frequently Challenged Books of 2006."

Challenges, Censorship, and This Book

What exactly is a challenge to a book? The American Library Association (ALA), founded in 1876, monitors challenges and defines a book challenge as a "formal, written complaint filed with a library or school requesting that materials be removed because of content or appropriateness." According to the ALA, there were 546 book challenges in 2006, an increase of 30 percent from 2005. The organization considers that number in "the midrange," and rather low compared to the peak years of the mid-1990s, when book challenges numbered more than 750 annually. Some experts attribute the surge at that time to the appearance of the *Harry Potter* series, one of the most challenged book series of all time.

Why does the ALA care about these challenges and monitor them so closely? "One of the things we believe is that materials need to be available to people so that they can make their own choices," former associate director of the ALA's Office for Intellectual Freedom Cynthia Robinson has said. "Removing books suppresses that point of view.... The First Amendment is very important to librarians and one of our most important rights as Americans. It's so fundamental I think people often take it for granted ... supporting intellectual freedom [and] the right of individuals and their families to decide what they're going to read is one of the association's most important missions and by far one of its most public."

Most book challenges noted by the ALA are made initially by parents of students who become aware of a book's content when their child brings it home to read or study. In many cases these challengers reject the honest depiction of the real world—and the language and behavior of those who inhabit it. Some adults do not care for their children to know what life is like in the netherworld of the drug addict or behind the locked gates of a boys' reformatory or a psychiatric hospital. Other challenges arise over the very issues that the authors are challenging and criticizing, such as physical or sexual child abuse, racism, and bullying in schools. Still other critics resent the proposition put forth in a number of these books that it is largely the system—whether school administrators, misguided parents, or corrupt governments—that is to blame for the injustices depicted. They are disturbed by the authors' sharp criticism of authority in all its forms.

When a formal challenge is made, the school district takes it seriously. In most cases, the school board or school superintendent will turn the matter over to a special review committee for consideration. The committee may already be established, but in many cases may only be formed when needed. The committee members may include school administrators, media specialists, teachers, parents, area residents, and even students. The challenged book may continue to remain in use in the school or in circulation in the school library while the committee is deliberating, although in some cases the book is removed during this period.

After reading the challenged book, possibly hearing more from the challengers, and discussing the matter among themselves, the committee members come up with a recommendation that is passed on to the school board. The school board then meets to consider the recommendation and votes to either accept the recommendation as it is or make another decision about the challenged book. Sometimes the school superintendent will play an important role in this decision.

Many challenges are rejected. According to Judith Krug, director of ALA's Office for Intellectual Freedom, only 30 out of the 546 challenged books were actually banned in 2006. These bans can take several forms. Some result in the complete removal of a book from the classroom and school library. In other cases, the book is taken from the classroom but is retained on the school library shelves, sometimes with limited access to certain grades or to be borrowed only with written parental permission. In still other cases, the challenged book is removed from one grade but taught in a higher grade where it is considered more appropriate.

Some book challenges are questionable or even absurd. In one case, parents in McKinleyville, California, challenged the joke book *Laugh Lines* in 1990 and wanted it removed from the elementary school library. The challenge claimed it was "demeaning" toward readers who read the riddles and couldn't come up with the correct answers. Other challenges are trivial. One parent, noted in a "Landmark Challenge" in this series, complained about the single use of a swear word by a character in a novel. Some challenges are misguided. According to the ALA, the most challenged book in both 2006 and 2007 was the children's picture book *And Tango Makes Three*, the true story of two male penguins that raise a baby penguin without a female. Parents complained that the book promoted a homosexual lifestyle. The same book was praised by the ALA as one of the best picture books of 2006.

"So many adults are exhausting themselves worrying about other people corrupting their children with books, they're turning kids off to reading instead of turning them on," wrote Judy Blume in the introduction to a collection of stories by banned writers. "In this age of censorship I mourn the loss of books that will never be written, I mourn the voices that will be silenced—writers' voices, teachers' voices, students' voices—and all because of fear."

The most important part of this volume is not the description of the challenges themselves but that of the courageous voices that rose up in opposition, to support these books and to defend them. In many cases they made the difference—ending a challenge or bringing a banned book back into the classroom or back on to the library shelf. These books are a cry for tolerance and justice in our world. They stand up for diversity and the differences that make us each unique individuals. If we deny ourselves their wisdom, wit, and power, we will all end up as the ultimate outsiders—estranged from one another, society, and ourselves.

The format of this book is straightforward. Each entry covers a single banned or challenged book, presented in chronological order by date of publication. Entries start with a brief, concise summary of the book in the "What Happens in" section. This is followed by "Challenges and Censorship," which may include some or all of the following: the history of how the author came to write the book, its initial reception from reviewers and readers, and the main reasons why it has been challenged in schools. Next is one or more "Landmark Challenges" described in detail. Some landmark challenges include several related challenges. Finally, each entry concludes with a list of sources for "Further Reading" and a brief biography of the author or authors in "About the Author of."

Why a series about book banning? Can we learn something from these cases of challenges and censorship of fiction? The American Library Association thinks so, which is why it reports on challenges from around the nation and the world in its monthly *Newsletter on Intellectual Freedom*, a publication now more than a half century old. The ALA also sponsors Banned Books Week each year to focus attention on books that have been banned.

"Throughout history, there always have been a few people who don't want information to be freely available. And this is still true," said ALA president Leslie Burger during Banned Books Week 2006. "The reason more books aren't banned is because community residents—with librarians, teachers, and journalists—stand up and speak out for their freedom to read." As long as we all recognize censorship when it arises and speak out against it, that freedom will remain secure.

The Outsiders (1967)
by S. E. Hinton

· · · · · · · · · · · · · ·

What Happens in *The Outsiders*

The two rival teen groups in a small Midwestern town are the working-class "greasers" and the upper-class "Socs" (Socials). The greaser Darry Curtis's parents are dead, so he's a surrogate father to his two brothers, 14-year-old Ponyboy, the novel's central character and narrator, and 16-year-old Soda, who is a garage mechanic.

Ponyboy and his pal Johnny Cade meet two girls, Cherry and Marcia, at a drive-in movie and fall in love. The girls are Socs, however, and the meeting leads to a fight in which Johnny stabs and kills one of the Soc guys. Dallas, another greaser, helps the two friends hide out in an abandoned church. When a fire breaks out in the church, the three greasers rescue children trapped inside and become heroes.

There is an inevitable rumble between the greasers and the Socs, which the greasers win, although Johnny is killed in the fighting. Dallas becomes depressed at his friend's death and forces a police officer to shoot him. Ponyboy is the survivor who finds release from his pain by writing about his dead brother and friend.

Challenges and Censorship

With the publication of *The Outsiders*, S. E. Hinton made one of the most auspicious debuts in the world of young-adult fiction. "At an age when most youngsters are still writing 300-word compositions, she has produced a book alive with the fresh dialogue of her contemporaries," wrote Thomas Fleming in the *New York Times*, "and has wound around it a story that captures, in vivid patches, at least, a rather unnerving slice of teen-age America."

Despite good reviews, the book did not become a best seller overnight. Hinton's first royalty check was only $10. According to the author, it was the support and enthusiasm of teachers and librarians that eventually made the novel a rousing success.

It was a picture of teen America that had rarely if ever been depicted in a book before. As Hinton said in one interview, "At the time, there wasn't any realistic fiction about teenagers. I wanted to read something that dealt with what I saw kids really doing." But the book's uncompromising realism did not please some parents and school administrators. Their challenges were largely based on the foul language and antisocial behavior of many of the characters. In Milwaukee, Wisconsin, the book was challenged for being "too negative" in its grim portrayal of teens from broken homes abusing drugs and alcohol.

"Teachers tell me that when a parent complains, they ask them to read the book themselves," Hinton has said. "Afterwards, there are no complaints." Optimistic words, but not exactly true. *The Outsiders* ranked forty-third on the American Library Association's "100 Most Frequently Challenged Books of 1990–2000." It is the only one of her novels to have made the list.

A fortieth-anniversary edition of *The Outsiders* was published in 2007. The novel by that year had sold more than thirteen million copies. "I get letters from all over the world, saying, 'It changed my life,'" Hinton said in a recent interview. "Who am I to change somebody's life? It's not me. It's in the book."

Landmark Challenge:
Hallucinating in Eleanor, West Virginia

Many challenged books have been charged with having negative effects on children, but perhaps none so unique as that made by Mildred Thornton against *The Outsiders* in Eleanor, West Virginia, in May 2000. According to Thornton, her fourteen-year-old son started to experience hallucinations after reading the Hinton novel at George Washington Middle School. He suffered from attention deficit disorder (ADD), and she claimed she had to increase his medication for the condition after reading the book. Thornton told the Putnam County school board that she wanted *The Outsiders* removed from the school library.

"A gang in the '50s [as depicted in the novel] is not a gang in the '90s," said George Washington principal Hershel Facemyer, defending the book at a school board meeting soon after Thornton's challenge. "The book tries to show kids who read it that there are consequences to bad decisions." Rather than subvert adult authority, Facemyer insisted, the author pointed out that there are times when young people need to turn to adults for help.

School board president Sid Linville explained that if Thornton hadn't wanted her son to read the book, all she had to do was request that he be allowed to read another, more acceptable book. Thornton responded that she did not know about the novel and its negative effects until after her son had already read it. The hallucinations did not begin until two months after he had read the novel, she claimed.

Pat Homberg, director of exceptional education in Putnam County, explained that the needs of Thornton's son could be further discussed at the next educational-needs meeting, but Thornton would not wait for that. She removed her son from the school and had him taught at home so he would not be exposed to another violent book that could upset him.

Further Reading

Fleming, Thomas. "Teenage Fiction" (book review). *New York Times*, May 7, 1967, International Economic Survey Section: 10, 12.

"Interview with S. E. Hinton." Barnesandnoble.com. Available online: http://search.barnesandnoble.com/booksearch/isbninquiry.asp?z=y &btob=I&isbn=014038572X#ITV. Accessed October 18, 2007.

Italie, Hillel. "Inside *The Outsiders*: Author Reflects on Her Novel 40 Years Later." *Connecticut Post*, October 6, 2007: D14.

Thomas, Clint. "GWMS Principal Defends Hinton Novel." *Charleston Gazette*, May 12, 2000: PO2.

Young Adult Library Services Association. *Hit List for Young Adults 2: Frequently Challenged Books*. Chicago: American Library Association, 2002.

About the Author of *The Outsiders*

S. E. Hinton (1948–)

Susan Eloise Hinton was born on July 22, 1948, in Tulsa, Oklahoma. Her father was a salesman and her mother worked in a factory. She loved to read as a child, but while attending Will Rogers High School she was disappointed with most young-adult books. She felt they didn't relate to her life and those of the people she knew in high school. At age 15, Hinton, who once received a "D" in creative writing, began to write the novel that would become *The Outsiders*. At 17, she submitted her manuscript to a New York literary agent, and it was published soon after her high school graduation. Because the book was violent and realistic and dealt mostly with the world of boys' gangs, her publisher, Viking Press, convinced Hinton to use only her first two initials on the title page so readers wouldn't know that she was female.

With the profits from her first novel, Hinton put herself through the University of Tulsa, earning a degree in education in 1970. That same year she married her college sweetheart, David Inhofe, who today is a mathematician and computer scientist. A second novel about two conflicted brothers, *That Was Then, This Is Now*, appeared in 1971 and brought back Ponyboy, the narrator of *The Outsiders*, as a minor character. This book was followed by two more novels about alienated youth, *Rumble Fish* (1975) and *Tex* (1979). All four of these novels were made into successful movies, two of them directed by Francis Ford Coppola, with Hinton serving as consultant.

She did not publish another novel until *Taming the Star Runner* in 1988. That year Hinton was the recipient of the first Margaret A. Edwards Award, presented by the American Library Association's Young Adult Services Division and *School Library Journal*, for her body of work. Hinton published two children's picture books in 1995; her first adult novel, *Hawkes Harbor*, appeared in 2004.

"I understand kids and I really like them," she has said. "And I have a very good memory. I remember exactly what it was like to be a teenager that nobody listened to or paid attention to or wanted around."

The Pigman (1968)
by Paul Zindel

• • • • • • • • • • • • •

What Happens in *The Pigman*

High school sophomores John Conlon and Lorraine Jensen both come from dysfunctional homes where they find little comfort. They are drawn into a friendship with an older man, Angelo Pignati, who doesn't judge them the way their parents do. They call him "the Pigman" because of the huge collection of decorative pigs that he shows them when he invites them over. His house becomes a second home to the two young people, one they enjoy being in far more than their real homes.

One day Angelo suffers a heart attack and goes into the hospital. While he is away, John and Lorraine watch his house for him. Enjoying this freedom, they throw a party in Angelo's house for their friends, and things quickly get out of hand. The partygoers wreck the house and Angelo's precious pig collection is destroyed.

Angelo arrives home from the hospital a day earlier than expected and finds the damage. Filled with shame and guilt, the two teens express their apologies, but it is too late. They later meet Angelo at the zoo, a favorite meeting place, where he learns his favorite animal, Bobo the baboon, has died of pneumonia. Angelo dies of a second heart attack at the zoo. John and Lorraine express their sorrow and guilt in the book we are reading, their "memorial epic" to their dear friend.

Challenges and Censorship

The Pigman, like many of Paul Zindel's best novels, came out of painful, personal experience. Growing up in a dysfunctional family on Staten Island, in New York, Zindel had his own "pigman," or adult mentor. He even wrote a childhood memoir about his experiences, *The Pigman and Me* (1992), as well as a sequel to the novel, *The Pigman's Legacy* (1980).

Critics praised *The Pigman*, which launched Zindel's career as a leading young-adult novelist. However, the book has drawn fire from many parents and school administrators. It ranked forty-fourth on the American Library Association's "100 Most Frequently Challenged Books of 1990–2000." Most of the challenges focus on bad language and the behavior of the two central characters. A 1985 challenge in Hillsboro, Missouri, claimed that the novel promoted "liars, cheaters, and stealers." A 1992 challenge in Lynchburg, Virginia, complained of no less than 21 instances in *The Pigman* of "destructive, disrespectful, antisocial, and illegal behavior . . . placed in a humorous light, making it seem acceptable."

Landmark Challenges: Protesting the "Dirty Stuff" in New Hampshire and New York

Challenges focusing on foul language are a frequent occurrence in schools, but in two cases in the early 1970s, they failed to remove *The Pigman* from the curriculum.

In October 1973 parents of students in the junior high school of Dover, New Hampshire, challenged the book for dialogue that included words such as "slut." Principal Timothy Gormley defended the book, calling it "interesting and well thought through" and said it gave students the opportunity to discuss in class important issues about human relations. William Purcell, leader of the challenging parents, saw it differently. "I see no sense in the language they [the book's characters] use," he said in reply. "There are a lot of children who have never heard the word 'slut.' They do hear some language down here [at the junior high school] no doubt about it, but I don't expect the teachers to teach it."

A second challenge in May 1974 in North Syracuse, New York, made it past the principal to a review committee appointed by the local school board. The challenge was made against *The Pigman* and three other books used in the local high school curriculum—the novels *The Catcher in the Rye*, by J. D. Salinger, and *Flowers for Algernon*, by Daniel Keyes, and the nonfiction book *Soul on Ice*, by African-American radical Eldridge Cleaver. The review committee, after careful deliberation, rejected the challenge and recommended retaining all four books as curricular materials. Upset parents responded that the committee "was not representative of the lay community." They insisted the books were filled with "filthy sexual language," singling out *Flowers for Algernon* and *Soul on Ice* as "beyond the limits which the community at large, if they read the books, would want for our children." Do we want, in the words of Rev. Jed. S. Snyder, a leader in the protest, "this dirty stuff given to these children"? But the challenge failed and the books remained.

Further Reading

"Dover, New Hampshire." *Newsletter on Intellectual Freedom*, January 1974: 9.

"North Syracuse, New York." *Newsletter on Intellectual Freedom*, July 1974: 81.

Paul Zindel official Web site. Available online: www.paulzindel.com. Accessed October 17, 2007.

Young Adult Library Services Association. *Hit List for Young Adults 2: Frequently Challenged Books*. Chicago: American Library Association, 2002.

About the Author of *The Pigman*

Paul Zindel (1936–2003)

Paul Zindel won acclaim as both a young-adult novelist and a playwright, writing about lost and lonely characters who were often drawn from his own life. He was born on May 15, 1936, on Staten Island, a borough of New York City. His father was a police officer who abandoned the family when Paul was very young. He was raised by his mother, a nurse. A loving but unstable woman, she was always falling for get-rich-quick schemes, and the family moved frequently. Zindel attended Wagner College on Staten Island, where he majored in chemistry. After graduating, he worked six months as a chemist at Allied Chemical and then quit to become a high school science teacher.

Zindel had been writing plays since his teens. In 1965 he completed a drama/comedy with the unlikely title *The Effect of Gamma Rays on Man-in-the-Moon Marigolds*. This semi-autobiographical play was produced on Broadway in 1971 and won the Pulitzer

Prize for Drama that year. None of Zindel's subsequent plays, which include *And Miss Reardon Drinks a Little* (1971) and *Ladies at the Alamo* (1977), have approached the popularity of his first one. In 1968 Zindel produced his first young-adult novel, *The Pigman*. Its success led him to write full time; over the next 35 years he published 39 books. Like Robert Cormier, Zindel wrote fiction that was often dark, with happy endings rare. The darkness was partly alleviated, however, by a wild sense of humor that is reflected in the titles of such novels as *My Darling, My Hamburger* (1969), *Pardon Me, You're Stepping On My Eyeball!* (1976), and *Confessions of a Teenage Baboon* (1977). In later years, Zindel turned to writing more formula fiction for younger readers, including the Wacky Facts Lunch Bunch series.

Zindel married novelist Bonnie Hildebrand in 1973. They had two children: Lizabeth, a novelist, playwright, and actress; and David, a filmmaker. The couple divorced in 1998. Paul Zindel died of cancer on March 27, 2003, at age 66.

"I try to show teens they aren't alone," Zindel once wrote. "I believe I must convince my readers that I am on their side; I know it's a continuous battle to get through the years between twelve and twenty—an abrasive time. And so I write always from their own point of view."

The Bluest Eye (1970)
by Toni Morrison

● ● ● ● ● ● ● ● ● ● ● ● ●

What Happens in *The Bluest Eye*

Eleven-year-old Pecola Breedlove is a poor black girl growing up in Lorain, Ohio, in 1941. She is looked down on and despised by not only whites but also blacks. One black schoolmate brings Pecola home to tease her with his mother's cat. He kills the cat and then, when his middle-class mother arrives home, blames the cat's death on Pecola. His mother is all too ready to believe him and throws Pecola out of the house.

Pecola's dream is to be a pretty little white girl like the child actress Shirley Temple. She longs to have the blondest hair and the bluest eyes. The hopelessness of this dream is starkly clear when Pecola's no-good father, Cholly, rapes and impregnates her.

In desperation, Pecola goes to Soaphead Church, an old man who supposedly has magical powers. She asks him to give her blue eyes. Soaphead tells her that her wish will come true if she feeds his landlady's dog some food, which he has secretly poisoned. When the dog dies, Pecola believes the old man has given her blue eyes. Later, she miscarries her baby and goes mad, telling herself over and over that she has the bluest eyes in the world.

The story is told from the perspective of five different characters, including Cholly Breedlove, two black sisters who befriend Pecola, and Soaphead Church.

Challenges and Censorship

Noble Prize–winning author Toni Morrison's first novel, *The Bluest Eye*, was inspired by an elementary schoolmate of Morrison's who wanted blue eyes like the white children. "*The Bluest Eye* was my effort to say something about that; something about why she had not, or possibly never would have, the experience of what she possessed and also why she prayed for so radical an alteration," wrote Morrison in an afterword to a 1993 edition of the novel. "Implict in her desire was racial self-loathing. And twenty years later I was still wondering about how one learns that. Who told her? Who made her feel that it was better to be a freak than who she was? Who had looked at her and found her so wanting, so small a weight on the beauty scale? The novel pecks away at the gaze that condemned her."

On its first appearance in 1970, the book received generally good reviews. "*The Bluest Eye* is . . . history, sociology, folklore, nightmare and music," wrote John Leonard in the *New York Times*. "It is one thing to state that we have institutionalized waste, that children suffocate under mountains of merchandised lies. It is another thing to demonstrate that waste, to re-create those children, to live and die by it. Miss Morrison's angry sadness overwhelms."

The book remains a stark document of both racial prejudice and the self-hatred it can breed in the young. "Along with the idea of romantic love, she [Pecola, the protagonist] was introduced to another—physical beauty," writes Morrison in her novel. "Probably the most destructive ideas in the history of human thought. Both originated in envy, thrived in insecurity, and ended in disillusion."

Probably Morrison's most widely read novel in high school curriculums, due in part to its short length, *The Bluest Eye* is also the most challenged of her eight novels. It ranked thirty-ninth on the American Library Association's "100 Most Frequently Challenged Books of 1990–2000." Many of the challenges focus on explicit sexual scenes, especially the shocking rape of Pecola by her father. Two other Morrison novels are also on the ALA list, *Beloved* (forty-second place) and *Song of Solomon* (eighty-fifth place).

A stage version of *The Bluest Eye*, written by Lydia R. Diamond, premiered at the Steppenwolf Theatre Company in Chicago in 2005.

Landmark Challenge:
A Superintendent in the Hot Seat

Too many times a superintendent of schools has stepped in and reversed a recommendation from a school board or review committee and supported a book ban. The opposite took place in Bakersfield,

California, in December 2003, when superintendent Bill Hatcher defended *The Bluest Eye* and found himself up against the district's board of trustees and an angry group of parents. It all started a month earlier when 16-year-old Sarah Porter, a student at East Bakersfield High School, brought the Toni Morrison novel home. She told her mother that the book's graphic descriptions of sex made her decidedly uncomfortable. Sue Porter perused the novel and agreed that the book's focus on pedophilic activity and incest was inappropriate for high school students. She filed a complaint with the school district, prompting Hatcher to call for a review committee to examine the complaint and make its recommendation.

In early December the committee reported back to Hatcher. "It [*The Bluest Eye*] is neither prurient not titillating," stated the committee. "More importantly, taken as a whole, it has serious literary value." It did add, however, that parents should be notified by letter before the book was taught, and if they were opposed to the book, their child could request an alternate reading assignment.

Hatcher declared on December 18 that the book would be available only to juniors and seniors in advanced English and honors classes. It would also be available in the school library for anyone who wanted to read it.

On January 12, 2004, at a board of education meeting, two school trustees questioned Hatcher's decision and asked that the board consider removing the novel from all high school classrooms. After more than a half hour of debate between challengers and supporters of Morrison's novel, board member and local farmer Larry Starrh took the floor. He said he had read the book and other background material and did not believe it was appropriate in any classroom. "I would like to recommend that we overrule the superintendent," Starrh declared. The item was placed on the agenda for the next meeting, to be held February 2.

Meanwhile, the Porters were continuing to wage their own battle against the book. They filed a lawsuit against Jean Nilssen, their daughter's English teacher, accusing her of sexual harassment for assigning *The Bluest Eye* to her eleventh-grade students. Sue Porter also formed the Citizens for Good School Books, a parents' group that sought to review other classroom novels in the Kern High School District. "I hope that people see a parent who is concerned that all of the children in our high school district are given good quality literature to read," she said. "That is my goal."

But there were many other people in the community who saw that goal as misguided. They included students, other parents, and even faculty members at California State University, Bakersfield. The university's Academic Senate issued a statement that supported superintendent Hatcher and said, "as university faculty, we have an obligation to protect freedom and to guard against undue censorship."

On February 2 the boardroom of the district's main office was filled with people hours before the meeting was scheduled to begin. Many of those present were teachers who supported Hatcher. The teachers' union even delivered a truckload of pizza for those who had skipped dinner at home to arrive early to get a seat. Just next door, the members of Porter's Citizens for Good School Books were gathering. Unable to gain entrance to the closed meeting, they were prepared to watch every moment on a television screen via a live feed.

When the meeting finally convened, both supporters and detractors of the novel spoke out passionately. "My daughter's experience [reading the novel] was one of the most profound literary experiences of her lifetime," said parent Kathy Yniquez. On the opposing side was pastor Chad Vegas, who boldly declared, "The teacher is not the sovereign over the students. The parents are."

When the speakers were done, the moment of truth had come. Trustee Larry Starrh made a motion to suspend the district's review process, paving the way for the banning of *The Bluest Eye*. Silence filled the boardroom as he waited for a second to his motion. None of the four remaining trustees would support Starrh, and the motion died on the floor. Trustee Sam Thomas, who had previously expressed his concern about the book, would not thwart the process that had been established. "We are not educators," he admitted. "The educators are the ones we put confidence in."

Hatcher's decision stood. "I think education won tonight," said the superintendent. "I think the open discussion of opinions and ideas won tonight." For Sue Porter and her followers, the battle was lost, but the war had just begun. "Our only protection was the elected school board and they failed us tonight," she said. " . . . I think they have no integrity. They state that this book was no good for their homes but that my child would have to opt out." She added she was seriously considering running for the school board.

Landmark Challenge: Little Hope in Littleton

When a study group at Heritage High School in Littleton, Colorado, recommended moving the controversial *The Bluest Eye* from an optional reading list to restricted use by only juniors and seniors, the group members thought they had solved the problem of those opposing the novel. But they were wrong. At an August 2005 meeting, the school board rejected their recommendation and ordered the removal of the novel from all school reading lists.

Teachers, librarians, and students were incensed by the action and spoke out in defense of the book at a special October 5 board meeting. "It's pretty shocking that any school board would ban a book by a Nobel Prize winner," said Littleton High School English teacher Judy Vlasin. "It's a huge step backward for the school district."

But others who spoke saw it as a step in the right direction. "Do they [students] need to know the explicit graphicness [sic] of a rape?" said parent Pam Cirbo. "I don't think so." She said the novel was only appropriate for reading by college-age students.

Arapahoe High School English teacher Marlys Ferrill disagreed. She urged her daughter, when she was a junior at the school, to read Morrison's novel. "I thought it was a very powerful way to for her to learn about the different issues people face in life," she said.

Camille Okoren, a Heritage High senior, saw a bigger problem with the banning. "Once you ban one book, parents and teachers think it's OK to ban another book," she said. "Everyone is offended by different things." Okoren and other Heritage High students participated earlier in a public reading of *The Bluest Eye* at the school library.

Some school officials saw the debate, while it did not alter the board's original decision, as productive nonetheless. "This is the kind of academic debate where we want our students engaged," said Mollie McDonald, director of curriculum instruction and assessment for Littleton Public Schools system. According to school board president Mary McGlone, any member of the community can bring up the issue of adding a book to the approved district reading list in the future.

Landmark Challenge: One Author Against Another

Ann Blaine and Toni Morrison are both novelists who write about women and their problems. But there the similarities end. Ann Blaine, a Mormon convert, is the author of *Sisters of My Heart*, a novel with a strong Christian theme. Morrison is African American, the author of eight novels, and the winner of the Nobel Prize in Literature.

When Blaine read several paragraphs from Morrison's *The Bluest Eye* before a standing-room-only crowd at a meeting of the Howell, Michigan, school board in early 2007, she was not doing so out of admiration for the author's prose. "Tell me, what is the redeeming quality of this book?" she asked the board members. "I've never read such smut like that in my life." The other novel being challenged in Howell schools was also by an African-American author—Richard Wright's semi-autobiographical *Black Boy*, published in 1945.

Blaine was not alone in her condemnation of *The Bluest Eye*. The Livingston Organization for Values in Education (LOVE) had strenuously opposed the novel before the board meeting. But another local group, the Livingston Diversity Council, defended it just as strenuously. "I hope [others outside of the community] don't look at this and say, 'Yep. That's Howell,'" said council president Steve Manor. "Every community goes through things like this; the conversations I've had with people seem to be there's a lot of people concerned about the tenor, the tone of all of this."

The controversy over the books spread to the office of U.S. Attorney Stephen J. Murphy III. Murphy referred *The Bluest Eye* and *Black Boy*, along with challenged books *Slaughterhouse-Five*, by Kurt Vonnegut, and *Running with Scissors*, by Augusten Burroughs, to the Federal Bureau of Investigation (FBI). He sought from them a decision as to whether the books were obscene, as alleged by LOVE. On March 7, 2007, Murphy announced that according to the FBI, neither "[t]he material submitted nor its inclusion as part of the school's required English curriculum constitutes a violation of federal law."

While applauding the U.S. Attorney and other officials for making "the right decision," Joan Bertin, executive director of the National Coalition Against Censorship, added that "the case demonstrates the need to educate more parents about how the First Amendment applies in public schools."

Further Reading

"Bakersfield, California." *Newsletter on Intellectual Freedom*, March 2004: 50–51. Available online: https://members.ala.org/nif/v53n2/dateline.html.

"Bakersfield, California." *Newsletter on Intellectual Freedom*, May 2004: 118–119. Available online: https://members.ala.org/nif/v53n3/success_stories.html.

"Free Speech Groups Welcome Decisions Clearing Challenged Books." National Coalition Against Censorship Web site, March 8, 2007. Available online: http://ncac.org/literature/20070308~MI-Howell~Free_Speech_Groups_Welcome_Decisions_Clearing_Challenged_Books. cfm. Accessed November 2, 2007.

"Howell, Michigan." *Newsletter on Intellectual Freedom*, March 2007. Available online: https://members.ala.org/nif/v56n2/dateline.html. Accessed November 21, 2007.

"Littleton, Colorado." *Newsletter on Intellectual Freedom*, January 2006. Available online: https://members.ala.org/nif/v55n1/dateline.html. Accessed November 21, 2007.

About the Author of *The Bluest Eye*

Toni Morrison (1931–)

The first African-American woman to win the Nobel Prize for Literature, Toni Morrison is one of America's most prominent living novelists. She was born on February 18, 1931, in Lorain, Ohio, the second of four children. Her father was a welder who told her black folktales that had a great influence on her later writing. A voracious reader as a child, Morrison attended Howard University, graduating with a bachelor's degree in English in 1953. She earned a master's degree in English from Cornell University two years later.

Morrison became an English instructor, first at Texas Southern University in Houston and then at her alma mater, Howard University. In 1958 she married Harold Morrison, with whom she had two sons. After the couple divorced, Toni moved to Syracuse, New York, where she worked as a textbook editor. Soon after she moved to New York City and became an editor at Random House, where she edited the work of such well-known African-American authors as Angela Davis and Gayl Jones.

Morrison began writing her own fiction as part of a group of writers at Howard. Her first novel, *The Bluest Eye* (1970), evolved from a short story. Her second novel, *Sula* (1973), was nominated for a National Book Award. *Song of Solomon* (1977), an epic novel about slaves in the South, was the first volume by a black writer to be chosen as a main selection for the Book-of-the-Month Club since Richard Wright's *Native Son*, in 1940. Her fifth novel, *Beloved* (1987), won the Pulitzer Prize for Fiction and was adapted into a film in 1998 starring Oprah Winfrey and Danny Glover. Morrison was awarded the Nobel Prize for Literature in 1993. Since then she has published two novels, *Paradise* (1999) and *Love* (2003).

Toni Morrison held the Robert F. Goheen Chair in the Humanities at Princeton University, in New Jersey, from 1989 to 2006. She remains to this day an outspoken critic of racism in America.

Go Ask Alice (1971)
by Anonymous

What Happens in *Go Ask Alice*

Go Ask Alice is the grim story, told in diary form, of a nameless 15-year-old girl's descent into drug abuse and a life of degradation. The "Alice" of the title refers to a line from a song about drug use by the rock group Jefferson Airplane. The book's narrator comes from a good, middle-class family, but a breakup with a boyfriend destroys her self-esteem. At a party, unbeknownst to her, she is given the drug LSD in a drink. Enjoying the experience, she becomes a regular drug user, starting with marijuana and moving on to amphetamines and other pills. Desperate to fund her growing drug habit, she becomes a drug dealer, selling drugs to her friends in high school and even elementary school students.

She eventually runs away to San Francisco, where she becomes addicted to heroin and is sexually abused by several men. She returns home to her parents, but then runs away again. On her second return home, she is determined to give up drugs and start her life over. But friends, fearing she will betray them, feed her candy laced with LSD. She experiences a bad "trip" and ends up for a time in a mental institution. The therapy she undergoes seems to work, and she returns to society confident that she can stay clean. She even decides to abandon her diary, which she sees as a crutch. But a chilling afterword to the book says that three weeks after this last entry, the girl was found dead of a drug overdose.

Challenges and Censorship

Although written as a cautionary tale to show young readers the consequences of drug use, *Go Ask Alice* has been challenged time and again by people who feel it has just the opposite effect. Reading it "would encourage experimentation by some individuals who would feel they could avoid the problems that the girl had in the book," stated a challenge in Nashotah, Wisconsin, in 1981. Other challenges have focused on the offensive language and many graphic references to drug abuse and sexual activity. According to a superintendent of schools in Wall Township, New Jersey, the book "borders on pornography." A parent in Pagosa Springs, Colorado, complained of its "immoral tone, and lack of literary quality."

Since its publication in 1971, *Go Ask Alice* has been successfully challenged and banned in many schools and school libraries nationwide. It ranked twenty-third on the American Library Association's "100 Most Frequently Challenged Books of 1990–2000." It was sixth on the ALA's "10 Most Frequently Challenged Books of 2003."

A best seller that still has the ability to shock, the book remains in print to date. A made-for-television movie adaptation was released in 1973 with Jamie Smith Jackson as the troubled protagonist and William Shatner and Julie Adams as her parents.

Landmark Challenges: The Banned Bookmobile and the Parents Who Had Second Thoughts

Two early 1980s challenges to *Go Ask Alice* stand out from the more humdrum run of book challenges.

A traveling bookmobile was a welcome sight at the Chester Elementary School in northwestern Wayne County, Ohio, which had a limited selection of books in its own school library. In April 1981, a bookmobile librarian recommended *Go Ask Alice* to the 11-year-old daughter of Carolyn Smith.

"She read two-thirds of the book before I came home," recalled Smith in a complaint to the school board. "When I got there, she gave me the book, I read it after she went to bed. It's a sad book, but it's not one that should be in the hands of a fifth-grader." In her complaint, Smith requested that the book's circulation be restricted to tenth graders and up. School superintendent Edward Shultz asked country librarian Joseph Marconi to remove the book from the bookmobile, but only on visits to schools in the northwestern district.

In 1982 *Go Ask Alice* was on a book list at the Safety Harbor Middle School library in St. Petersburg, Florida. But the 20-book list was called "mature," and students could borrow the book only with parental permission. Jackie Personett and her husband gave their sixth-grade daughter their permission to read the book. But they changed their minds after taking a look at *Go Ask Alice* for themselves. They found the book's language objectionable and filed a challenge with school authorities to have the book removed from the library's shelves. A book review committee, composed of two parents, three teachers, and a librarian, considered the complaint two weeks later and voted to keep the book. The Personetts did not appeal the committee's decision.

Landmark Challenge: Applying "Biblical Standards" in Hanover

English teacher Robert Parkis felt no qualms when he asked superintendent Clifford Easton to order more copies of *Go Ask Alice* for his sophomore literature class. After all, the popular book had been taught at South Shore Vocational Technical High School in Hanover, Massachusetts, for 13 years. But in all that time, Easton had never read the book. He did now—and was not pleased. He told Parkis to stop using the book in his classroom. According to Easton, "the language and the way the book is presented is [not] appropriate for this school."

Disturbed by Easton's decision, Parkis went to the school committee to appeal the matter. Parkis stressed that the book was a powerful teaching tool for his students. "This is the most moral book I know," he said. "It is as moral as the Bible. I honestly and truly believe this book can save a life."

The superintendent took issue with Parkis's reference to the Bible. "I have a Biblical standard, OK?" he said. "The problem with that is many people would not look upon that as an appropriate standard to use in a public school. I as the superintendent want to respect the entire spectrum of society. I try not to let my religious and moral convictions make decisions for me, but they are standards I have to live by and I let them help me decide."

While he objected strongly to the profanity in *Go Ask Alice*, this was not the only standard to which Easton said he held school materials. "If there was a book by homosexuals, or a book on sexual technique, or a book describing terrorism techniques, you think they would be on my library shelf? No way." A majority of the school committee apparently agreed with Easton. On December 11, 1985, they voted 4 to 3 to ban the book from the classroom. Under the superintendent's recommendation, however, the book remained in the school library. Easton felt leaving it in the library made it optional reading for students—but leaving it in the classroom implied that the school condoned it.

Landmark Challenge: The Police Chief's Daughter

Kristine Prout felt uneasy reading *Go Ask Alice* for a homework assignment in her ninth-grade English class at Shepherd Hill High School in Dudley, Massachusetts. She told her father, who happened to be the local police chief, about it. In May 1992, Chief William Prout decided to take action. He collected 176 signatures on a petition, condemning the book for its "gross and vulgar language and graphic description of drug use and sexual conduct." Among the most objectionable sexual passages, both father and daughter agreed, was one describing lesbian sex. "I just felt uncomfortable reading it. Maybe if it was for a health class," said Kristine.

A review committee was authorized to assess the petition and the book and to make a recommendation. Only one member, Shepherd Hill principal Alfred L. Thibaudeau, wanted the book removed. The majority found the book acceptable and recommended that it be retained in the curriculum.

But the school committee of the towns of Charlton and Dudley was more in agreement with Thibaudeau. In a 4 to 3 vote on June 8, 1994, the committee disregarded the review committee's recommendation and removed *Go Ask Alice* from the ninth-grade reading list. Two and a half years after making his initial complaint, Chief Prout was satisfied.

Landmark Challenge: Anonymous in Aledo, Texas

Most parents who challenge a book in their child's school are willing to stand up and be identified. But not in Aledo, Texas, in 1999. A parent whose daughter attended the local middle school complained about *Go Ask Alice*, but did so anonymously. The challenge attacked the book, which the daughter had borrowed from the school library, for its offensive language, sexual descriptions, and frequent references to drug use.

The anonymity of the challenger didn't phase the school board, which voted 3 to 1 to remove the book from the middle school library at a meeting on June 14, 1999. Board president Steve Reid wanted *Go Ask Alice* removed from the high school library as well, but his colleagues refused to take that step. "What purpose does this book serve in a learning environment?" asked Reid, who had not read the book. "I'm going to have a hard time being sold that this is a book for learning." The board did stipulate that a student would need parental permission before being allowed to borrow the book from the high school library.

Further Reading

"Aledo, Texas." *Newsletter on Intellectual Freedom*, August 1999: 2.

"Dudley, Massachusetts." *Newsletter on Intellectual Freedom*, September 1994: 150.

Foerstel, Herbert N. *Banned in the U.S.A.: A Reference Guide to Book Censorship in Schools and Public Libraries*. Westport, Conn.: Greenwood Press, 2002.

"Hanover, Massachusetts." *Newsletter on Intellectual Freedom*, March 1986: 41.

"Nashotah, Wisconsin." *Newsletter on Intellectual Freedom*, July 1981: 92.

"St. Petersburg, Florida." *Newsletter on Intellectual Freedom*, July 1982: 142.

Sova, Dawn B. *Banned Books: Literature Suppressed on Social Grounds*. New York: Facts On File, 2006.

"Trenton, New Jersey." *Newsletter on Intellectual Freedom*, May 1977: 73.

"Wayne County, Ohio." *Newsletter on Intellectual Freedom*, September 1981: 125.

About the Author of *Go Ask Alice*

Beatrice Sparks (1918–)

Go Ask Alice, purported to be the actual diary of a 15-year-old girl, was written, as the title page indicates, by "Anonymous." However, soon after the book was published, psychologist Beatrice Sparks identified herself as editor of the book. Since then, it has become clear that Sparks was the author of the work. The existence of any diary that she used as source material has been cast in doubt. Critics point out that the language and content of *Go Ask Alice* is not consistent with the diary of a teen girl. Sparks's inability to produce the original diary is also suspect. She claims to have destroyed part of the diary and had the remaining manuscript locked in a publisher's vault.

Beatrice Mathews Sparks was born on January 15, 1918, in Goldburg, Idaho. She studied psychology at the University of California at Los Angeles (UCLA) and Brigham Young University in Salt Lake City, Utah. In 1955 she began working with troubled teenagers as a music therapist at Utah State Mental Hospital. Her experiences inspired her to write what she calls "cautionary tales" to keep other young people from falling into the same traps as her patients.

After the commercial success of *Go Ask Alice*, Sparks published a string of similar books, purporting to be diaries of troubled youths. None achieved the popularity of *Go Ask Alice* and all were considered purely fiction. The first of these, *Jay's Journal* (1978), was surrounded in controversy. The mother of a 16-year-old Utah boy who had committed suicide gave Sparks his diary to edit and publish. When the book appeared, the mother was shocked. Sparks had used only a few of the diary entries and imposed, the mother claimed, the issue of Satanism onto her son's story, something she insisted had not existed. Sparks maintains that "Jay" was involved in Satanism, based on interviews she conducted with his friends.

Sparks's other works include *It Happened to Nancy: By an Anonymous Teenager* (1994), *Almost Lost: The True Story of an Anonymous Teenager's Life on the Streets* (1996), *Annie's Baby: The Diary of Anonymous, a Pregnant Teenager* (1998), and *Finding Katie: The Diary of Anonymous: A Teenager in Foster Care* (2005).

Summer of My German Soldier (1973)
by Bette Greene

• • • • • • • • • • • • •

What Happens in *Summer of My German Soldier*

The small town of Jenkinsville, Arkansas, seems far removed from the upheaval of World War II. But that changes when about 20 German prisoners-of-war arrive by train to be detained in a nearby prison camp. Twelve-year-old Jewish girl Patty Bergen befriends one of the prisoners, 22-year-old Anton Reiker, the only one of the Germans who speaks fluent English. Reiker is no stereotypical Nazi. He hates Hitler, Nazism, and the war and comes from a distinguished German family in Göttingen, where his great-grandfather was the president of the University of Göttingen.

Reiker fascinates lonely Patty. He treats her with the kindness and gentleness that she doesn't find at home. Her self-absorbed mother ignores her, and her mean-spirited father, who operates the town's department store, verbally and physically abuses her. Patty's only true friend is their black maid, Ruth, who loves her and accepts her for who she is.

Patty's relationship with Anton becomes more complicated when the German prisoner escapes from the camp. She gives him shelter and food as he plans his escape from Jenkinsville. Patty eventually involves Ruth in her secret relationship with Anton. When Patty is brutally beaten by her father for talking to a poor boy in the neighborhood, Anton nearly rushes to her assistance, despite the jeopardy it will put him in.

When Anton finally decides it is time to leave Arkansas and head east to New York, he gives Patty a valuable family heirloom, a gold ring. At first she refuses to take it, but then Anton tells her to always remember that "you have a friend who loved you enough to give you his most valued possession."

Patty foolishly wears the ring and then must explain to her father where she got it. She makes up a story about a tramp giving her the ring in return for some food, and her father suspects that this stranger molested her. But Patty sticks to her story and is believed by the local sheriff, who is far more understanding than her own father.

Later, a special agent for the FBI interviews Patty about the "tramp" and reveals that Anton was shot and killed in New York City while trying to elude capture. Distraught at this news, Patty explodes with anger and passion, revealing that she did indeed know Anton and helped him escape capture. Patty is put on trial, and she and her family are vilified as Jews and Nazi lovers.

The more serious charges against Patty are eventually dropped, but she is still sentenced to six months in a state reformatory for girls. Her only visitor in the reformatory is the faithful Ruth, who has been fired from her job working for the Bergens. Ruth's love and support give Patty the courage to carry on. As Ruth leaves after a visit, Patty considers the difficult road before her. "For moments or minutes I stood there," she tells us. "Not really moving. Barely managing to tread water. Was it possible for a beginning swimmer to actually make it to shore? It might take one a whole lifetime to find out."

Challenges and Censorship

Summer of My German Soldier was Bette Greene's first novel for young adults. It took her five years to complete; she spent another two years looking for a publisher. After 18 rejections, the novel was published by Dial Press in 1973.

The book earned mostly praiseworthy reviews. The *New York Times Book Review* hailed it as "an exceptionally fine novel" and named it an Outstanding Book of the Year. The critic for *Horn Book* called it a "moving first novel, unforgettable because of the genuine emotion it evokes." The American Library Association named *Summer of My German Soldier* a Notable Book, and in 1973 it was a National Book Award Finalist. In the years since its publication, the book has become a classic novel for young readers.

But initial response was not universally positive. Reviewer Audrey Laski in the *New York Times Educational Supplement* felt that the novel would "disturb a reader as young as its twelve-year-old heroine, because of the domestic violence . . . it records." Others criticized Greene for making the captured German a hero and Mr. Bergen, the central Jewish character, one of the book's central villains. "I'm Jewish, proudly Jewish," Greene responded, "but that doesn't mean that I'm incapable of writing about a flawed human being who happened to be Jewish."

Such criticisms have led to numerous book challenges in schools and school libraries. Challenges have focused on the occasional use of bad language, including several references to "niggers" by townspeople, as well as sexual references. The sex is mainly in Patty's head, since she shares nothing more with Anton than an innocent kiss.

Summer of My German Soldier ranked eighty-ninth on the American Library Association's "100 Most Frequently Challenged Books of 1990–2000." It also came in fifth place on the ALA's "10 Most Frequently Challenged Books of 2001."

The novel was adapted into an Emmy Award–winning made-for-television movie in 1978, starring Kristy McNichol as Patty, Bruce Davison as Anton, and Esther Rolle as Ruth. That same year Greene published a sequel, *Morning Is a Long Time Coming.* It picks up Patty's story when she is 18 years old and leaves home to travel to Germany to find Anton's mother.

Landmark Challenge: Big Deal in Burlington

Summer of My German Soldier was just one of four books and a short story that parents Donna and Charles Beach of Harwinton, Connecticut, wanted dropped from the Har-Bur Middle School reading list in November 1990. The books—which included Paul Zindel's *The Pigman*, Robert Newton Peck's *A Day No Pigs Would Die*, and Robert Cormier's *The Chocolate War*—were full of obscenities and negativity, according to the Beaches. Worst of all, they undermined the authority of teachers and parents. Also under fire was Cormier's short story "In the Heat."

The complaint was considered by an 11-member curriculum committee of Region 10 in Burlington. After due deliberation, on February 5 the committee concluded to retain all of the books and the story. The vote was unanimous. "These five books are highly acclaimed across the nation and have received high distinction for their literary merit," declared Warren Baird, committee chairperson. "The teachers really look closely at the groups and whether the books are appropriate for their kids in a group at a given time," said Anne Malley, a teachers' representative.

Committee member Ann Bailey spoke even more forcefully in defense of the books. "Students who have struggled with painful experiences will gain a clearer perspective of themselves in the bigger picture," she said. "They need a compelling view of the world. These books do that."

While the board commended the Beaches for speaking up for what they believed, members also cautioned parents not to overstep their rights as individuals. "Parents should not have the right to dictate the curriculum for the entire school or a particular grade level," said middle school teacher Emily Perretta. "One set of parents does not have a right to determine what other children will read."

Landmark Challenge: Censoring the "N" Word in Cinnaminson

It wasn't anti-Semitism or the portrayal of a sympathetic German soldier that brought a successful challenge against *Summer of My German Soldier* in Cinnaminson, New Jersey, in 1996. It was black racial stereotypes. Never mind that Ruth, the Bergens' African-American servant and Patty's confidant, is one of the most admirable characters in the novel. The whites in this 1940s segregated Southern town refer to her and other blacks as "Nigra," "darky," and worse. This bothered a number of African-American parents whose children were assigned the book in middle school, and they complained to the school board.

The board agreed to temporarily remove the book from the supplemental reading list for eighth graders. "My position is simply that any time a book is going to be introduced in the district that it is sensitive to any child, and when there is no groundwork for teaching that book, then that book should not be used," said Elease Greene-Smith, an African-American member of the board. The local branch of the National Association for the Advancement of Colored People (NAACP) also got involved in the case. "We want to sit down and talk with these people [teachers teaching the book] because something's amiss," said Roosevelt Nesmith, coordinator of the Southern Region,

New Jersey Conference of the NAACP. Officials in the school system promised to make changes in the district curriculum policy on the approval of all reading materials.

Further Reading

"Bette Greene." Biography.jrank.org. Available online: http://biography. jrank.org/pages/1660/Greene-Bette-1934.html. Accessed November 7, 2007.

"Burlington, Connecticut." *Newsletter on Intellectual Freedom*, May 1991: 90.

"Cinnaminson, New Jersey." *Newsletter on Intellectual Freedom*, January 1997: 10.

About the Author of
Summer of My German Soldier

Bette Greene (1934–   )

Bette Evensky Greene was born on June 28, 1934, in Memphis, Tennessee, and experienced prejudice firsthand in childhood. Shortly after she was born, her parents moved to a small town in Arkansas, not unlike Jenkinsville in *Summer of My German Soldier*. As the only Jewish family in town, the Evenskys always felt like outsiders.

Greene took to writing early in her life and, at age nine, sold her first news story—about a barn fire—to a Memphis newspaper for 18 cents. When she was about 14 her family moved back to Memphis, where she graduated from high school in 1952. She went on to attend several colleges and universities without earning a degree from any of them.

Greene continued to write while employed as an information officer for the American Red Cross and then for the Boston State Psychiatric Hospital. She married Donald Greene, a Boston physician, in 1959. The couple settled in the Boston suburb of Brookline and raised two children.

Her first young-adult novel, *Summer of My German Soldier* (1973), remains her best-known work. Among her other books are *Philip Hall Likes Me, I Reckon Maybe* (1974); *Get On Out of Here, Philip Hall* (1981); and *I've Already Forgotten Your Name, Philip Hall!* (2004), a popular series for middle-grade readers about fourth grader Beth Lambert and her friend and rival Philip Hall.

Greene hopes her books, especially her young-adult novels about prejudice and intolerance, will change lives. "Again and again, I see a lot of physical courage, but so little moral courage," she has said. "I see young people who will do all kinds of physical things to save people they don't know, but they will do little or nothing to save a friend if they have to stand up and say 'Leave this person alone.'"

The Chocolate War (1974)
by Robert Cormier
• • • • • • • • • • • • •

What Happens in *The Chocolate War*

Freshman Jerry Renault is doing his best to fit in at all-boys' Catholic Trinity High School. He tries out for the football team and makes it, despite his thin build. But there are forces of conformity that begin to press in on Jerry and cause him to become an outsider and a victim.

Brother Leon, the temporary head of the school, wants each student to sell 50 boxes of chocolates as a fundraiser. The sale is especially urgent because Leon has used school money without permission to buy the chocolates and must sell them all or risk ruining his reputation. He turns to Archie Costello, leader of the Vigils, an underground student gang, to support the chocolate sale. Archie agrees, but at the same time is at cross-purposes with Leon's policies. The Vigils give "assignments" to freshmen that are often cruel pranks at the school's expense. Jerry's assignment is to refuse to sell the chocolates. Each day, Brother Leon reads from the roll call of student sales and each day Jerry says "no" to selling even one box.

After 10 days, according to his assignment, Jerry is supposed to give in and say "yes." But he decides not to. What started out as a prank has become a deliberate act of individual rebellion. At first, Jerry's nonconformist stance gains him the support and admiration of other students, but as Leon puts pressure on the Vigils, the students turn against Jerry. Under Archie's direction, Emil Janza, a school bully, aided by his underlings, gives Jerry a beating. But Jerry refuses to be intimidated. He stays true to the poster in his locker that urges him to dare to "disturb the universe."

The sale ends as a resounding success for Brother Leon. However, 50 boxes of chocolates, Jerry's share, remain unsold. Archie persuades Jerry to take part in a showdown in which he will box with Emil before a gathering of students in the football stadium. As Brother Leon watches approvingly, and the other students call for blood, Emil beats Jerry to a pulp. Another brother breaks up the fight, but Jerry is seriously injured. Before he is taken away in an ambulance, he tells his one remaining friend, Goober, that perhaps it isn't such a good idea to disturb the universe, and that maybe it is better to "play the game" and not make waves.

Challenges and Censorship

Robert Cormier had published three adult novels before *The Chocolate War* and had every intention of aiming this book at the adult market as well. His agent, however, thought it would be better marketed as a young-adult novel since it dealt almost exclusively with life among students in a Catholic high school. Of the first publishers the manuscript was submitted to, one felt it was neither a young-adult nor an adult book, but something in between. Three other publishers wanted Cormier to change the downbeat ending, giving the novel a more hopeful conclusion. But Cormier couldn't bring himself to do it, and all three publishers refused the book. Finally, Pantheon Books agreed to publish *The Chocolate War* as written, and it came out in 1974.

The book was the most critically acclaimed young-adult novel of the year. The *New York Times* called *The Chocolate War* "masterfully structured and rich in theme" and named it one of the Best Books of 1974. The American Library Association (ALA) gave the book its prestigious Margaret A. Edwards Award and deemed it one of the "classics in young adult literature."

But there were a few dissenters, including *Booklist*, which claimed it was too cynical and undermined moral values. A war of censorship soon began over the book among parents, administrators, and teachers who agreed with this assessment. Frequent attacks have made *The Chocolate War* one of the most challenged books in schools and school libraries since its publication. It ranked fourth on the ALA's "100 Most Frequently Challenged Books of 1990–2000" and first on the ALA's "10 Most Frequently Challenged Books of 2004."

Most challenges have centered on four issues—profanity, violence, sexual references (especially to homosexuality), and a questioning of the church's and school's moral authority. While Archie and his Vigils are shown in a negative light, the blackest villain in the novel is Brother Leon, the school's head, whose cold cruelty is exposed numerous times. Perhaps the most graphic example is when Leon sadistically victimizes a top student who has done nothing wrong in front of the class and then accuses the other students of not standing up for the victim. *The Chocolate War*, according to one challenger in Cornwall, New York, in 1985, "starts with evil, is evil throughout, and is evil to the end."

Cormier wrote a sequel, *Beyond the Chocolate War* (1985), which saw Archie Costello's leadership in the Vigils challenged and again pitted Jerry Renault against the forces of conformity at Trinity School. *Children's Book Review Service* called it "a brilliant sequel, more finely crafted, denser in plotting, and more subtle in character nuance than at his [Cormier's] debut ten years ago as a YA author."

Landmark Challenge:
A "Community Compromise" in Columbia

Two district review committees in Columbia, South Carolina, found *The Chocolate War* suitable for middle school students, but a challenge from a local minister changed all that. In 1984 the Reverend Ronald LaFlam complained about the more than 130 obscenities he cited in the Cormier novel. The school board acted accordingly, overruling the two review committees' findings. "Due to pervasive vulgarity, this book is educationally unsuitable and inappropriate for the maturity levels of students in grade six, seven, and eight," the board stated.

District teachers and librarians were not pleased. "This is definitely a blatant case of book banning and censorship," responded librarian Melinda Hare. "I think parents in the district who are concerned about children's right to read will also speak out now." South Carolina American Civil Liberties Union (ACLU) executive director Melissa Metcalfe called the decision "absolutely outrageous" and announced her organization would file a suit against the school district.

The showdown came on June 26, 1984, when more than 150 people attended a school board meeting, two-thirds of them voicing their opposition to the book banning. After all had spoken, the school board met in a closed executive session. They reached what they called "a community compromise." Eighth graders would be allowed access to *The Chocolate War*, but no younger students in the middle schools could borrow it.

The compromise was accepted, though not wholeheartedly by all. "How do you isolate a single book?" asked director of Spring Valley High School's media center Laura Jackson. "Are they going to keep it under lock and key? [The decision] is not in keeping with the idea of intellectual freedom, [and] is, in essence, the same thing as banning it."

Landmark Challenge: Pursuing an R-Rated Book in West Hartford, Connecticut

If Rick and Donna Stockwell had their way, every questionable book for middle and high school students would be rated PG-13 or R, just like the movies. And the biggest R rating would be reserved for *The Chocolate War*, a book they spent more than a year attempting to get removed from the middle schools of West Hartford, Connecticut.

It all started in the fall of 2005, when the Stockwells' eighth-grade son came home from King Philip Middle School with the novel, which he had been assigned in his language arts class. His mother, Donna, had heard the book was controversial and sat down to read it. Disturbed by what she read, she gave the novel to her husband, Rick, to read. "I just thought to myself, 'do I really want this material going into my son's mind, and later on into my daughter's mind,'" said Rick Stockwell after finishing the book.

Donna Stockwell contacted her son's teacher, Jessica Kerelejza, who had taught the novel at least three times in the past. Kerelejza politely listened to Stockwell's complaint, but refused to drop the novel from the class. She suggested that the Stockwells' son could read an alternative book if he chose to.

This wasn't the answer that Donna Stockwell wanted to hear, and she took her complaint to Kerry Meehan, supervisor of the English department. He defended *The Chocolate War* more vigorously than Kerlejza. "It's probably one of the best young-adult novels that's been written," he wrote the couple in an e-mail. The Stockwells responded that perhaps just as films were rated for young audiences, curriculum books should be rated PG-13 and R for readers.

The Stockwells next turned to King Philip principal Mary Hourdequin. In a long letter written on October 27, they listed the offensive language and sexually explicit references in the book. Hourdequin sent them an inquiry form, which the Stockwells sent on to Dr. Karen List, assistant superintendent for curriculum and instruction. She in turn sent the inquiry to a special committee of teachers for evaluation. A month later, she informed the Stockwells of the committee's verdict: *The Chocolate War* would stay in the curriculum. But the Stockwells weren't ready to give up their fight yet.

On December 6 they delivered a letter to school board chairman Jack Darcey during a board meeting. The letter presented their challenge against the Cormier novel, while also requesting the establishment of a book rating system that would require parental permission for books rated PG-13 and R.

"The basic concept here is the board does not really get involved in all of our textbooks and reading materials because we really don't have the expertise to make judgments," Darcey wrote in a March 10 letter to the Stockwells.

The Stockwells decided it was time to let other parents know of the frustration they were experiencing. Over two nights, the couple copied and mailed 375 letters to all eighth-grade parents at King Philip. Their letter received only 10 responses, eight of them favorable to their challenge. A meeting soon followed with the Stockwells, several other parents, and the principal and Meehan. They pressed again for a committee of parents and faculty to make decisions on books like *The Chocolate War*.

"It's not going to be easy," said Rick Stockwell. "but they have to develop some kind of standards in terms of profanity, sexual content, and violence. . . . The schools should be a place where we raise the bar a higher standard; we shouldn't be dumbing down our curriculum to mesh with pop culture." As for his son, he had chosen to read an alternative to the assigned book in question—*The Outsiders*, another frequently challenged young-adult novel.

Landmark Challenge:
Harassing a Novel in Harford County, Maryland

In August 2006, parents of freshmen at high schools in Harford County, Maryland, received the syllabus being taught in a new social studies class. Called "Living in a Contemporary World," the goal of the class was to aid students in making the transition from middle school to high school. In a unit on harassment and bullying, students would read Robert Cormier's award-winning novel *The Chocolate War*. Several parents who perused the book were not impressed. They found the novel subversive to authority and felt it was more likely to promote bullying rather than prevent it. By the fall, school officials were being inundated with complaints in the form of e-mails and phone calls. The protest to get the book removed from the curriculum came to a head at a school board meeting in September.

"When I spoke at the board meeting last year," recalled parent and Army officer John Wagner, "I said [that] we don't tell our children to go out at midnight because nothing good can come from it. Offering a controversial book as part of the curriculum seemed to be a similar situation."

George Toepfer, supervisor of social studies for county schools, defended his decision to include the novel in the curriculum. "I knew going into it that the book was controversial," he said. "It's a dark novel because at the end, the good guys don't seem to win. But I thought it had a strong lesson to teach students."

A review committee made up of teachers, administrators, librarians, and parents was formed to consider the challenges. While they deliberated, the book was pulled from the classroom. The committee's report recommended *The Chocolate War* be retained. "The educational value of the novel outweighs any concerns about language and graphic scenes," the report stated. "Teaching this novel in no way condones the evil portrayed or the language used. . . . The book prompts a discussion of morality and everyone's human responsibility to stand up against cruelty and evil." The report emphasized that the complaints against the novel came from a small, but outspoken, group of parents.

But this group had found a sympathetic ear in superintendent of schools Jacqueline Haas. In April 2007 she announced to the Board of Education that, despite the review committee's recommendation, she was pulling it from the ninth-grade curriculum. "The controversy that has occurred over *The Chocolate War* has left it unusable at this time," Haas wrote on the schools' Web site. "While the superintendent would want to make the decision . . . on the merits of the book, the divergent views of this work make it difficult to continue its use at this time."

A number of parents reacted negatively to Haas's decision. "I was disappointed and angry when I heard [it]," said Laura Krebs, who had three children in school. "I don't think [Haas] put a lot of faith in the parents who made the decision to let their children read the book. It allows for discussion, and no good comes from not talking about something."

A letter of protest was sent to the superintendent from the executive director of the National Coalition Against Censorship and other groups. "Without questioning the sincerity of those seeking removal of the book, their views are not shared by all, and they have no right to impose those views on others or to demand that the educational program reflect their personal preferences," the letter stated. "... We strongly urge you to restore this book to ninth-grade classrooms. In our experience, controversies of this sort are best handled by enriching the curriculum, not restricting it, and by including additional voices rather than silencing any."

But Haas did not back down on the ban. The bullying unit was dropped from the course for the 2006–07 school year, and a suitable alternative to *The Chocolate War* was sought for the new school year. The ban, however, did not remove the book from school and public libraries in Harford County. The controversy actually made the novel in demand in the library system. "We had so many people reading the book that we had to order more copies," said Jennifer Ralston, material management administrator for county public libraries.

Further Reading

"Columbia, South Carolina." *Newsletter on Intellectual Freedom*, September 1984: 138.

"Cornwall, New York." *Newsletter on Intellectual Freedom*, March 1985: 45.

Foerstel, Herbert N. *Banned in the U.S.A.: A Reference Guide to Book Censorship in Schools and Public Libraries*. Westport, Conn.: Greenwood Press, 2002.

"Harford County, Maryland." *Newsletter on Intellectual Freedom*, July 2007. Available online: https://members.ala.org/nif/v56n4/dateline. html. Accessed November 21, 2007.

"Joint Letter to Harford County Superintendent About Removal of *The Chocolate War* From Ninth Grade Curriculum." National Coalition Against Censorship Web site, April 18, 2007. Available online:

www.ncac.org/literature/20070418~MD-HarfordCounty~Joint_
Letter_To_Harford_Superintendent_Protesting_Removal_Of_The_
Chocolate_War.cfm. Accessed October 27, 2007.

Santoni, Matthew. "'Chocolate War' to Be Cut from Harford Schools'
Curriculum." Examiner.com, April 9, 2007. Available online: www.
examiner.com/a-663446~'Chocolate_War'_to_be_cut_from_
Harford_schools'_curriculum.html. Accessed October 27, 2007.

"West Hartford, Connecticut." Newsletter on Intellectual Freedom, July
2006: 184–185. Available online: https://members.ala.org/nif/v55n4/
dateline.html.

Young Adult Library Services Association. Hit List: Frequently Challenged Books for Young Adults. Chicago: American Library Association, 1996.

About the Author of *The Chocolate War*

Robert Cormier (1925–2000)

Robert Cormier is considered by many critics and readers to be the finest young-adult author in America. In his unforgettable novels and stories he fearlessly plumbs the depths of good and evil and explores the corruption of the world and its values. He was born into a French-Canadian family in Leominster, Massachusetts, where he lived all his life. He attended parochial primary and secondary schools and had his first literary efforts, several poems, published in the *Leominster Daily Enterprise*, a newspaper. Cormier attended Fitchburg State College, where a professor submitted his story "The Little Things That Count" to a Catholic magazine that published it and paid the author $75.

After a two-year stint writing scripts and commercials for a Worcester, Massachusetts, radio station, Cormier became a local reporter for the *Worcester Telegram & Gazette*. He became well known in the region for his weekly human-interest column "A Story from the Country." In 1955 he moved to the *Fitchburg Sentinel*, where he covered city hall and local politics.

In 1960 Cormier published the first of three well-received adult novels. Then *The Chocolate War* (1974) became a huge success and established Cormier as a major writer for young adults. He followed it with the equally popular *I Am the Cheese* (1977) and *After the First Death* (1979). In 1980 he received the coveted Margaret A. Edwards

Award for young-adult literature. The award cited these three works as "brilliantly crafted and troubling novels that have achieved the status of classics in Young Adult literature."

Cormier's other works include the story collection *8 Plus 1* (1980), *The Bumblebee Flies Anyway* (1983), *We All Fall Down* (1991), *Tunes for Bears to Dance To* (1992), and *Tenderness* (1997). His last novel, *Frenchtown Summer* (1999), won the Los Angeles Times Book Prize for Young Adult Fiction in 2000.

Robert Cormier died on November 2, 2000, at age 75. In an interview shortly before his death, he said, "My dream was to be known as a writer and to be able to produce at least one book that would be read by people. That dream came true with the publication of my first novel—and all the rest has been a sweet bonus."

Blubber (1974)
by Judy Blume

What Happens in *Blubber*

Fifth-grader Linda Fischer has the misfortune to be slightly over-weight. Because of this, her classmates, led by the popular Wendy, make fun of her. After Linda gives a report in class on whales, Wendy's clique starts calling her Blubber. Among Linda's harassers is Jill Brenner, the narrator and protagonist of the novel. Things become more serious when the harassers, urged on by Wendy, strip Linda in the girls' restroom and force her to eat chocolate ants. Jill turns against Wendy and stands up for Linda during a mock trial.

Jill now is the one who is ostracized and harassed. Wendy extends the harassment to Jill's best friend, Tracy Wu, who is Chinese American. She makes a racial slur against Tracy, which only makes Jill all the more determined to fight her. Ironically, Linda, herself a victim, now joins in the harassment of Jill, eager to be accepted by Wendy and her followers.

In the end, Jill triumphs in a showdown in the girls' restroom, although Wendy is not entirely put in her place. Jill extends a hand of friendship to a new girl, Rochelle. As for poor Linda, the title character, she remains alone and still the target of the bullies.

Challenges and Censorship

Blubber is one of four Judy Blume books to make the American Library Association's "100 Most Frequently Challenged Books of 1990–2000." It ranked in thirty-second place, below *Forever* (eighth place), but well above *Deenie* (forty-sixth place) and *Are You There God? It's Me, Margaret* (sixty-second place).

Blume got the idea for the novel from an incident in her daughter Randy's fifth-grade class. The novel's sharp critique of bullying in school has won it widespread praise, but not everyone has seen its realistic depiction as positive. Some challengers of the book have insisted that rather than discouraging bullying, *Blubber*'s graphic view of it and its appeal may actually incite children to become bullies. They also point out that while Wendy, the ringleader, is brought down a notch by the book's end, she escapes any real punishment for her despicable behavior. Other challenges to *Blubber* have been based on offensive language, violence, sexual references, and the triumph of evil over good.

"When I began this book I was determined to write the truth about the school-bus culture in the language of that culture," Blume writes on her Web site. "*Blubber* is funny to a point, then wham! Some adults are bothered by the language and the cruelty, but the kids get it. They live it. In some places the book is used in teacher training classes to help future teachers understand classroom dynamics."

Landmark Challenge:
Double Trouble in Xenia, Ohio

Anti-Christian. Subverting parental authority. Encouraging drug use and sexual activity. These were some of the charges leveled against *Blubber* and three other young-adult books by a group of parents whose children attended Spring Valley Elementary School in Xenia, Ohio. On June 13, 1983, about 50 residents attended the Xenia Board of Education meeting to hear arguments for and against the books, which included another Blume novel, *Are You There God? It's Me, Margaret*, along with Shel Silverstein's *Where the Sidewalk Ends* and Louise Fitzhugh's *Harriet the Spy*.

Bill Dean, one of the challengers, read excerpts from each book. The excerpt from *Blubber* included a student calling a teacher a "bitch," a clear sign for Dean of the author's attempt to undermine authority. He accused *Are You There God? It's Me, Margaret* of mocking God and Christianity.

But there were those parents who defended the books. "Students should be taught how to read and write and reason, not what to read or write or think," said Marilyn McKeown. "There should be moral guidance from parents. You are responsible for your own child, not your neighbor's."

"Being black, I could go to the library and find many books I find offensive," pointed out Malcolm Lewis, Jr. "My children must have an understanding with each and every thing in this world in order that they do not become plowed under."

After listening to parents and other residents speak for an hour, the board decided to put off any final decision on the books until their August meeting. They planned to read and review the books in question before that. No more has been heard from them.

Landmark Challenge: "Evil Triumphant" in Perry, Ohio

"There are so many uplifting, positive things they could be reading. Why choose to dwell on something entirely negative?" parent Brent Burner asked the Perry, Ohio, school board in a challenge to *Blubber* in 1991. "[B]ad is never punished. Good never comes to the fore. Evil is triumphant. There's no use hoping the teachers can save you; they can't. They're fools."

Burner, whose daughter was in fourth grade at Whipple School, wanted the novel removed from all elementary school libraries. The parent's challenge was brought before a district review committee. In early December 1991, the committee rejected his challenge. "When you get to the higher ethical meaning, the book does have a redeeming message," said the school's curriculum director Elaine Trevelli, a member of the review committee. "The theme would be one of individualism and the fact that differences occur in people, and an understanding that not all children are alike."

When he came before the school board to make his appeal, Burner found a more sympathetic listener in board president Chuck Stewart. "I think the book should be trashed," Stewart remarked. "I don't think there's a thing redeeming about the book."

Unfortunately for Burner, Stewart was later replaced as board president by Irene Splittorf, who was not so sympathetic. On March 24, 1992, the board voted unanimously to return *Blubber* to school libraries. "No one is being forced to read [*Blubber*], but no one is being denied the chance," said Splittorf. "The right to read this book should be protected, yet a parent also has a right to monitor his own child's reading. That does not give him the right to monitor other children's reading."

Further Reading

Foerstel, Herbert N. *Banned in the U.S.A.: A Reference Guide to Book Censorship in Schools and Public Libraries.* Westport, Conn.: Greenwood Press, 2002.

"Peoria, Illinois." *Newsletter on Intellectual Freedom,* January 1985: 8.

"Perry, Ohio." *Newsletter on Intellectual Freedom,* July 1992: 124.

"Perry Township, Ohio." *Newsletter on Intellectual Freedom,* March 1992: 41.

"A Split Decision: Judy Blume in Peoria." *Newsletter on Intellectual Freedom,* March 1985: 33, 58.

"Xenia, Ohio." *Newsletter on Intellectual Freedom,* September 1983: 139.

About the Author of *Blubber*

Judy Blume (1938–   )

No contemporary young-adult author's books have been challenged and censored as frequently as those written by Judy Blume. She has been a pioneer in writing about the problems and feelings of growing adolescents that had previously been overlooked or ignored in children's literature.

She was born Judy Sussman on February 12, 1938, in Elizabeth, New Jersey. After attending the only all-girls public high school in the state, where she was a feature editor for the school newspaper, she enrolled at New York University (NYU) and earned a bachelor's degree in education in 1961. At the end of her junior year she married lawyer John Blume. The Blumes settled down in suburban New Jersey, where Judy became a housewife and mother to two children.

She still loved writing and was inspired after taking an NYU course in writing for children. Blume soon published her first work, a children's picture book. The middle-grade novel *Iggie's House* followed, and in 1970 her first young-adult novel, *Are You There God? It's Me, Margaret,* appeared. The latter is considered a pioneer in YA fiction for dealing honestly and candidly with issues that concerned adolescents, especially love and sex. Each subsequent novel broke new ground: *Deenie* (1973) was about a girl suffering from curvature of the spine; *Blubber* (1975) dealt with weight problems, peer pressure, and bullying; and *Forever* (1975) charted a high school senior's first sexual relationship. Less controversial were Blume's middle-grade books, especially the best-selling *Fudge* series, which has been adapted for television and the musical stage. Blume's books have sold more than 70 million copies to date and have been translated into 26 languages.

Blume speaks out often against censorship of her books and those of fellow authors and is a supporter of the National Coalition Against Censorship and other watchdog organizations. She is concerned with the steady increase in challenges in school libraries and classrooms since the 1980s. "I feel badly for the children because it sends a message to them that there is something wrong with reading," she has said, "that we don't want them to read this book because there's something in it that we don't want them to know."

I Am the Cheese (1977)
by Robert Cormier
• • • • • • • • • • • •

What Happens in *I Am the Cheese*

As the novel opens, Adam Farmer, a troubled teen, is riding his old-fashioned bicycle from his home in Monument, Massachusetts, to Rutterburg, Vermont, where his father is recovering from an accident in a hospital. As he rides he sings the song "The Farmer in the Dell," which his father used to sing to him. Interspersed with Adam's long and eventful ride to Vermont are a series of taped transcripts of interrogations between Adam and a seemingly empathetic psychiatrist named Brint, who is trying to help him regain his memory. As the interrogations go on, Adam begins to piece together a troubled, forgotten past. His father had been an investigative reporter who uncovered a scandal involving the government and organized crime. After his father testified at a trial, the whole family was relocated and given different names and lives by the government. His father finally tells Adam the truth of their past and he learns that his real name is Paul Delmonte.

Back in the present, Adam/Paul faces numerous trials and obstacles on his journey to Rutterburg. He is nearly bitten by a terrifying dog, is threatened by three young hoods in a car who force him and his bike into a gully, and briefly loses his bike to a thief in Hookset, Vermont. As Adam draws closer to Rutterburg, he recalls the terrible accident in which a car ran them down on the road near the Canadian border. His mother was killed and his father injured and separated from him.

As Adam arrives at the hospital he sees the dog, the hoods, and other people he has met along the way. The reader realizes that the entire bike ride was taking place in Adam's imagination, and that this whole time he has been in the hospital himself in a drug-induced dream. It is here that the interrogations have been taking place. Not only is Adam's father dead, but Adam himself may soon be "terminated," in the cold, bureaucratic language of the government agents, when he has no more useful information to give them. The book ends with the dream starting again and Adam on his bike pedaling toward Rutterburg.

Challenges and Censorship

I Am the Cheese, with its shadowy government conspiracy that is never fully revealed and its terribly grim ending (grim even for Robert Cormier), is nonetheless free of most of the questionable content that motivates many book challenges in schools. There is little "foul language," the briefest references to sex, and only sporadic violence. From its publication in 1977 until 1987, the novel faced virtually no challenges or other attempts at censorship.

Then, in 1986, there were three well-publicized challenges, all of which succeeded in getting the novel removed from schools and school libraries. What these challenges, as well as subsequent ones, found most objectionable about the book was the idea that the American system of government could be so corrupt and menacing as to terrorize and kill people like Paul Delmonte and his family for uncovering criminal activity. The fact that Cormier never explains what this activity is makes it all the more disturbing.

The book initially appeared in the post-Watergate era, when many Americans could easily believe that their government was capable of conspiracy and lies. In 1986 the Reagan presidency was nearing its end, and the country was in a more conservative mood. George Bush, Reagan's vice president, won the presidential election of 1988, and the first Gulf War soon followed. A renewed sense of patriotism may well have made readers react more negatively to Cormier's novel. As one challenger at Cornwall High School in New York stated in 1985, I Am the Cheese is "humanistic and destructive of religious and moral beliefs and of national spirit."

Landmark Challenge:
The Five-Year Challenge in Panama City

The elaborate web of deception in which Adam Farmer finds himself trapped in I Am the Cheese was no less bewildering to many residents of Panama City, Florida, than the challenge over the book which took five long years to resolve.

It all started in April 1986, when Marian Collins, the grandmother of a Mowat Junior High School student, sent a letter to the superintendent of schools, Leonard Hall. She asked him to remove the book from the curriculum for its offensive language and support of humanism. Superintendent Hall told Mowat principal Joel Creel to remove the book at once.

But subsequently, Collins insisted that the book was still in use in the school. English teacher ReLeah Hawks had taken matters into her own hands and offered an alternative text to students whose parents were opposed to the Cormier book. She received only four requests for the alternate book out of 92 students.

Superintendent Hall again ordered *I Am the Cheese* removed from classes, along with *About David*, a novel by Susan Pfeffer. At the same time, a district review committee was formed and given the charge to consider the challenge. A month later the committee recommended that *I Am the Cheese* be returned to the classroom. But Hall held his ground and refused to reinstate the book. He found staunch support among the Collinses and other parents. Charles Collins, Marian's husband, sent a letter detailing the novel's "subversive theme" to parents of all students. He and others bought ads in the local newspaper soliciting phone calls to the school board to affirm the banning.

The response from the teachers and parents who opposed the banning was just as strong. They held a public meeting on May 27 to discuss the issue. Superintendent Hall ordered teachers to tell their students that they could not attend the meeting. Of the 300 parents who did attend the meeting, about 200 of them supported the teachers.

On June 5, Hall publicly stated his disdain for the book and its message of government corruption. "The mother and father are exterminated by the U.S. government," he said. "What does that tell you? I mean do you ever trust government again?"

For many teachers it was their administrators that they decided they couldn't trust. Hall put forth a new five-step procedure that all school materials, except for state-approved textbooks, had to go through to become curriculum. If the material failed to meet the criteria, Hall said, there would be no appeals process. At an August 1986 school board meeting, 17 citizens spoke out against the new policy. Nevertheless, the board approved the new policy, adding a one-year grace period for any materials taught in the 1985–86 school year. When teacher Gloria T. Pipkin, the chairman of the school English department, made a request to teach *I Am the Cheese*, it was rejected. Pipkin tried again and was again turned down. She appeared before the next school board meeting. The chairman attempted to prevent her from speaking, but could not. "Make no mistake about it," Pipkin declared, "*I Am the Cheese* has been banned in the Bay County school system because the ideas it contains are offensive to a few: no ruse can obscure that fact."

At this point, Hall tightened the restrictions on approved materials. He created three categories for materials, ranging from "no vulgar, obscene, or sexually explicit material" to "quite a bit of vulgar or obscene and/or sexually explicit material." Under this draconian system, 64 books were eliminated from county schools. They included numerous literary classics such as *The Great Gatsby*, *The Red Badge of Courage*, *Animal Farm*, *Fahrenheit 451*, *Of Mice and Men*, and the play *A Raisin in the Sun*.

Public protest went into overdrive. A petition signed by about 2,000 residents was sent to the school board. High school students throughout the district protested by wearing black armbands when attending board meetings. Then on May 12, 1987, 44 Bay County parents, teachers, and students filed a suit against the school board, the superintendent, and principal Creel. The suit argued that Hall's review policy denied the First Amendment right of students to be educated and of teachers to have free speech. After more than a year of litigation, U.S. District Court Judge Roger Vinson handed down a decision that pleased neither side. He denied the board's motion to dismiss the suit, but found the school board within its rights to review materials.

When Hall decided to step down as superintendent and not run for reelection, the trial was suspended for 60 days for the benefit of his successor. In fact, the suspension stretched into three years. During this time a new, more acceptable book review policy was negotiated for teachers by People for the American Way, an organization opposed to censorship. The long challenge in Panama City was finally over.

Landmark Challenge:
A Change of Heart in Elko, Nevada

It's not unusual for a book challenge to be rejected unanimously by a school review committee. What is unusual is when the parent making the challenge is a member of that committee and part of the unanimous vote.

When Courtney Welch, father of a 12-year-old student at Elko Junior High School in Nevada, first made his challenge concerning *I Am the Cheese* to the school board on November 30, 2004, he had no second thoughts. "I have a responsibility to my daughter to protect her from things that I feel are morally not correct for her at this time and age-inappropriate," he declared to the board. He wanted the novel removed from the seventh-grade honors English class, although he did not fully explain his objections to the book until later. It was, he said, the "sexual content and it alludes to other things I disagree with."

Marti DeLance, the honors English teacher, disagreed. "I always thought this book was perfect for teaching bright, well-motivated students," she said. "I think some things taken out of context completely skews people's opinion of the book. These few little incidents that are being found objectionable are not the main thing."

Another outspoken defender at the board meeting was longtime Elko resident Janice King. "Let us trust our teachers," she said. "If the school board or the administration begins banning some of the books that some groups find objectionable we create an atmosphere where teachers have their hands helplessly tied and teaching becomes secondary to placating small but vocal groups. Education should be first and foremost in the opening of minds and the teaching of critical thinking. This cannot occur if we try to place our children into a bubble where we allow no thought-provoking reading."

But Welch was adamant in his opposition to the book. "The damage is done to my daughter now," he stated. "My daughter has been exposed to this reading material, now we are picking up the pieces behind her." He then mentioned that he had three younger children who would soon be entering junior high. He wanted to remove the book to spare them.

Following district procedure, the school board formed a media review committee to look into the challenge. Among the nine people chosen to be on the committee were two parents, one of them being Courtney Welch. All members of the committee read the novel and met twice to discuss it. On January 18, 2005, the committee gave its report to the school board. All nine members, including Welch, recommended keeping *I Am the Cheese* in the honors English curriculum.

Welch's change of heart may have been partially motivated by a provision in the report that said teachers should let parents know in advance of books to be used in the classroom for the school year. "This will provide parents an opportunity to be more involved in their child's education by allowing them the chance to read books themselves before the books are read in class," the report stated.

While unanimous on the decision to keep the novel, there was some dissension among members on other issues. They disagreed on whether offensive language was appropriate to the book's purpose and whether questionable elements of the story were integral to the novel's message.

The consensus of the school board was that the review committee, including the book's challenger, did an excellent job. "I think the process worked very well," said school board member Annette Kerr.

Further Reading

"Elko, Nevada." *Newsletter on Intellectual Freedom*, January 2005: 9–10. Available online: https://members.ala.org/nif/v54n1/dateline.html.

Foerstel, Herbert N. *Banned in the U.S.A.: A Reference Guide to Book Censorship in Schools and Public Libraries*. Westport, Conn.: Greenwood Press, 2002.

Karolides, Nicholas J. *Banned Books: Literature Suppressed on Political Grounds*. New York: Facts On File, 2006.

Woodson, Dave. "Controversial Book Passes Muster." *Elko Daily Free Press*, January 19, 2005. Available online: www.elkodaily.com/articles/2005/01/19/education/education1.txt.

Young Adult Library Services Association. *Hit List: Frequently Challenged Books for Young Adults*. Chicago: American Library Association, 1996.

About the Author of *I Am the Cheese*

See biography in *The Chocolate War* entry.

Daughters of Eve (1979)
by Lois Duncan

· · · · · · · · · · · · ·

What Happens in *Daughters of Eve*

The Daughters of Eve is an exclusive national high school sorority known for its good deeds. But it takes a dark turn at Modesta High School when new advisor Irene Stark comes on the scene. Stark has a deep hatred of men, based on personal experience, and her feelings begin to rub off on the club members. Many of the girls already have their own issues with the men in their lives. Ruth Grange is forced by her parents to do all the housework at home while her three brothers have few domestic responsibilities. Jane Rheardon watches helplessly as her father abuses her mother, both verbally and physically. Laura Snow, overweight and lacking any self-confidence, quickly falls prey to Ruth's unscrupulous brother Peter after he breaks up with his steady, school beauty Bambi Ellis, who is also a member of the Daughters of Eve. Tammy Carncross, who appears to have psychic powers, is the only one of the girls in the club who senses trouble ahead when she sees blood dripping from a candle during the initiation ceremony for Laura and two other girls.

The plot goes into high gear after Peter heartlessly dumps Laura before the big homecoming dance and resumes his relationship with Bambi, taking her as his date instead. Distraught after Peter's brother Niles tells her the truth about Peter, Laura attempts suicide. When the club members learn about Peter's heartless treatment of Laura, they devise a chilling punishment. Under Irene Stark's direction, they lure Peter to a secluded spot in town, capture him, and shave the hair off his head.

The club strikes again when it believes, wrongly, that member Fran Schneider's science project has been rejected for the state science fair by a teacher who favors the inferior project of a male student. In retribution the girls destroy the boy's project and demolish the science lab. Irene Stark's influence becomes more damaging when she advises another student, pregnant Ann Whitten, who is engaged to the erstwhile David, to have an abortion rather than marry David and ruin her promising career as an artist. Ann ends up deciding to have the baby, but there is no happy ending for Jane Rheardon, whose pent-up anger against her abusive father leads her to unthinkable violence. Poor Jane ends up in a mental institute while Irene Stark's poisonous influence continues. In an afterward, we learn that three years later Stark is the school's vice principal.

Challenges and Censorship

When *Daughters of Eve* first appeared in 1979, it was highly praised by reviewers and was named a Best Book for Young Adults by the American Library Association. "[It is] finely constructed and told," said the *New York Time Book Review*, comparing the dangerous circle of girls in the novel to the tribe of unsupervised boy castaways in William Golding's novel *Lord of the Flies*. According to *Publishers Weekly*, "Duncan's latest thriller is as gripping and well told as its fine predecessors." "Duncan takes care to maintain an ideological balance with her offending males and her twisted feminists," observed the critic for *Kirkus Reviews*.

But that sense of twistedness and cruelty displayed by the central characters led to a number of challenges in schools. With the exception of one of the landmark challenges noted here and another in the middle schools of Fairfax, Virginia, most of the challenges failed in getting the novel banned from libraries and classrooms.

Landmark Challenge:
The Case of the Precocious Reader

Although she was only in the sixth grade, Amy and James Hendrick's daughter was reading at a high school level. And that where's the trouble began in 2005. Lowell Middle School in Lowell, Indiana, had a point system for required reading that motivated students. Each book read from the approved reading list had a point value, and the higher the reading level of the book, the more points the student would receive. At the end of the semester, students received rewards for the reading points they amassed. The Hendricks' daughter chose Lois Duncan's *Daughters of Eve* because it was at a difficult reading level and because, as her mother said, "She didn't want them [teachers] to think she wasn't reaching to their expectations."

But the book, the girl soon discovered, didn't live up to her expectations. She complained to her parents about the novel's bad language and its content, which dealt with such sensitive issues as abortion, spousal abuse, seduction, attempted suicide, and murder. When they brought their complaint to the school, a review committee considered the challenge, according to Ursula Andrews, assistant superintendent of curriculum. The committee felt that it was up to the student to ask for an alternative title before reading the book. Since she had not done so, the committee said no action would be taken.

"There are major, valuable lessons [in the book], but they are mature," admitted Andrews after reading the book. The school board took no action on the Hendricks' request that stickers alerting parents to the book's contents be adopted. The couple persisted in the belief that books like *Daughters of Eve* are not appropriate for sixth graders, regardless of students' reading abilities. "My daughter's age level and reading level do not coincide," said Amy Hendrick.

Landmark Challenge: Not So Clueless in Clovis

It's a rare event when a book banning is approved by the author of the book, but that's what happened in Clovis, New Mexico, in 2007. Donald Reid's fifth-grade grandson borrowed *Daughters of Eve* from the Zia Elementary School library. Although he never filed a formal complaint, Reid made known his feelings that the book was "not appropriate for a fifth-grade student."

Zia principal Jarilyn Butler brought the matter to school district officials. "We want parents to be confident that if their child chooses a book from our library, it is one that will be appropriate for their age level," she said. Clovis Municipal Schools Superintendent Rhonda Seidenwurm reviewed the book and complaint and decided to remove the book from all Clovis elementary schools, but not middle and high school libraries.

"Once in a while something slides through," Seidenwurm explained. "What I am not willing to do is remove a book from a library just because a particular person is upset about a particular thing."

Butler agreed with the decision, which she felt did not reflect negatively on Lois Duncan's book. "*To Kill a Mockingbird* is a great book, but it is not appropriate for elementary school students," she said. "We have to be vigilant."

Duncan herself, who lived for many years in New Mexico, had no complaint about the banning. "That's not an age-appropriate book for elementary school libraries," she said.

Further Reading

"Clovis, New Mexico." *Newsletter on Intellectual Freedom*, January 2007. Available online: https://members.ala.org/nif/v56n1/dateline.html. Accessed November 21, 2007.

"Lowell, Indiana." *Newsletter on Intellectual Freedom*, May 2005: 109–110. Available online: https://members.ala.org/nif/v54n3/dateline.html.

Stone, RoseEtta. "Interview with Lois Duncan." Absolute Write Web site. Available online: www.absolutewrite.com/specialty_writing/lois_duncan.htm. Accessed October 31, 2007.

About the Author of *Daughters of Eve*

Lois Duncan (1934–   )

For more than four decades, Lois Duncan has been among the outstanding young-adult authors of books of mystery and suspense. She was born Lois Duncan Steinmetz on April 28, 1934, in Philadelphia, Pennsylvania. Her parents were the well-known magazine photographers Joseph Janney and Lois Steinmetz. The family moved to Sarasota, Florida, when Lois was very young. She took to writing at an early age and sold her first story to a magazine when she was 13.

She attended Duke University in North Carolina for a year, but dropped out and married. While raising three children she continued to write, selling articles to such well-known magazines as *Redbook*, *McCall's*, and *Reader's Digest*. She eventually divorced her husband and moved to Albuquerque, New Mexico. She taught journalism at the University of New Mexico and met Don Arquette, whom she married in 1965.

The following year Duncan published her first young-adult mystery, *Ransom*. Her writing career took off with the publication of *I Know What You Did Last Summer* (1973), about a group of teens who kill a young boy in a hit-and-run accident. It was made into a movie in 1991. Although the film version was a hit, Duncan was not pleased with it, calling it a pointless slasher film and not worthy of her novel. Among her other novels of suspense are *Summer of Fear* (1976), *The Third Eye* (1984), *The Twisted Window* (1987), *Don't Look Behind You* (1989), and *Gallows Hill* (1997).

In 1989 Kaitlyn Arquette, her youngest child, was shot in Albuquerque while driving home. She died of her wounds the next day. The police called it a random drive-by shooting, but Duncan believed her daughter was targeted by a gang of criminals who was involved with Kaitlyn's estranged Vietnamese boyfriend. Duncan pursued the case on her own, hiring a private detective and psychic investigators. The story of her search for her daughter's killers is movingly told in *Who Killed My Daughter?* (1992). The case remains unsolved to date. Duncan's involvement in psychic investigation led her to cowrite *Psychic Connections* (1995) with William George Roll of the Psychical Research Foundation.

Duncan was the recipient in 1991 of the Margaret A. Edwards Award for lifetime achievement. "My primary message (I hope) is that reading is fun," Duncan has said. "Another underlying message, which seems to work its way into many of my books, is the importance of taking responsibility for one's own actions."

Annie on My Mind (1982)
by Nancy Garden

. . . .

What Happens in *Annie on My Mind*

Liza Winthrop and Annie Kenyon are teens with different back-grounds and interests, but when they meet by chance at the Met-ropolitan Museum of Art in New York City, it's friendship at first sight. Liza comes from an upper-middle-class family in prestigious Brooklyn Heights, attends a private school, and wants to go to the Massachusetts Institute of Technology (MIT) to study architecture. Annie's mother is a bookkeeper and her father a cab driver. They live in a poorer section of Brooklyn, where Annie attends public school. She dreams of going to college and pursuing a singing career.

The two girls become fast friends and enjoy each other's com-pany at their homes and on day trips. Gradually their friendship ripens into love. Annie knows she's gay, but Liza is just discovering her sexual orientation. The girls get the opportunity to explore their new relationship when two teachers from Liza's school go on vaca-tion and ask her to stay at their home and care for their cats. Annie joins Liza at the house, and together they discover a shelf of books on lesbianism in a bedroom. They conclude that the two teachers are lovers.

When Liza's school secretary discovers the girls alone in the house just before the two teachers return, she is suspicious. Then the teachers return home and there is trouble. The headmistress of the school attempts to get Liza expelled, but she fails. Ironically, the two teachers are fired, while the trauma of the situation dam-ages Annie and Liza's relationship. They leave for college—Liza to

MIT and Annie to Berkeley in California. On opposite coasts, there seems little hope that they will rekindle their love. Annie writes letters to Liza that go unanswered. Liza sits down and attempts to write Annie and finally gives up and calls her on the phone. They cry and tell each other "I love you," making plans to meet during the coming Christmas vacation.

Challenges and Censorship

When *Annie on My Mind* appeared in 1982 it was one of the first novels for young adults that dealt with the previously forbidden theme of lesbianism. Garden depicted the growing love between two teenage girls with sensitivity and a lack of sensationalism. Her message is best expressed by Ms. Widmer, one of the two lesbian teachers, who says to the girls, "Don't punish yourselves for people's ignorant reactions to what we all are." "Don't let ignorance win," adds her partner. "Let love."

The American Library Association designated *Annie on My Mind* a "Best of the Best Books for Young Adults" for the year. *School Library Journal* placed it on its list of the 100 most influential books of the twentieth century. But its subject matter drew numerous challenges in schools around the country. It ranked forty-eighth on the ALA's "100 Most Frequently Challenged Books of 1990–2000."

Nearly all the challenges focus on the theme of lesbianism. Author Nancy Garden has been accused of, among other things, portraying lesbian love as "normal" and promoting and encouraging a gay lifestyle.

In 1994 Garden collaborated with another writer on a stage adaptation of her novel. It was produced that November at the Renegade Theatre in Lawrence, Kansas, as part of the youth theater's "Banned Book Theatre." Protesters picketed the production.

Landmark Challenge:
"A Preposterous Case of Censorship"

Book donations to school librarians are usually welcome, but such was not the case in several San Ramon, California, high schools, where a gift of books set off a firestorm of controversy in 1990.

The books donated were *Annie on My Mind* and Frank Mosca's *All American Boys*, both novels dealing with homosexual teens. They were given to more than 20 high schools in Contra Costa County by the Bay Area Network of Gay and Lesbian Educators (BANGLE). Most of the school librarians accepted the books with thanks. Then Monte Vista High School vice principal Becky Smith asked school librarian Arla Stevens to let her have the books to examine them. That was the last Stevens saw of the books. She wrote two notes to Smith asking about the books and finally received a response in September that said "it may take some time to uncover and discover their location." Similar incidents occurred at San Ramon Valley High and California High, where vice principals took the books and never returned them.

When news of the disappearing books reached Rob Birle, a member of BANGLE, he was furious. "Whoever caused these books to not be on the shelves was just imposing their own political agenda in blatant violation of our values of free expression and thought," Birle said. "This is a preposterous case of censorship."

The charge of censorship was "ridiculous," according to Jerry Grundehoffer, director of secondary education for the district. "He [Birle] can't say it's censorship, he's not a part of our school community—he's not a teacher, he's not a resident, and he's not a parent."

But school librarians were equally outraged by the action. So was Margaret Crosby, an attorney with the American Civil Liberties Union (ACLU), who sharply criticized the school district on two counts. "One issue here is the sloppiness of the handling that went on," Crosby said. "The other issue is that a school district cannot exclude the topic of homosexuality from a school library."

Landmark Challenge:
A Book Burning in Kansas

When another gay rights group distributed copies of Garden's and Mosca's novels to Kansas City area school districts, the books didn't simply disappear—some of them were burned.

On October 23, 1993, a short time after Project 21 distributed the books, a group of protestors, led by a fundamentalist Christian minister, burned a copy of *Annie on My Mind* on the steps of the Kansas City School District headquarters. When author Nancy Garden was told of the burning by a reporter, she said, "I didn't think people burned books anymore. Only Nazis burn books."

The incident set off the burning of other copies in Kansas City high schools, but the district kept the books on school library shelves. Not so in Olathe, Kansas. There in December 1993, school superintendent Ron Winner ignored the positive review given *Annie* by high school librarians and ordered that the donated copies and previously owned copies be removed from the district's high school libraries. Winner's actions were supported by the school board, which voted 4 to 2 against keeping the books. Winner claimed he made the decision in part to "avoid controversy," including more book burnings.

The local head of the ACLU represented a number of parents, students, and teachers in a suit against the school district. The case went to trial in September 1995. Three months later, U.S. District Court Judge Thomas Van Bebber ruled in favor of the plaintiffs and ordered the books be returned to the school libraries. In his ruling, Van Bebber questioned the prosecution's charge of the books' "educational unsuitability."

"There is no basis in the record to believe that these Board members meant by 'educational suitability' anything other than their own disagreement with the ideas expressed in the book," the justice said. " . . . Accordingly, the court concludes that defendants removed *Annie on My Mind* because they disagreed with ideas expressed in the book and that this factor was the substantial motivation in their removal decision. . . . Defendants unconstitutionally sought to 'prescribe what shall be orthodox in politics, nationalism, religion, or other matters of opinion.'"

The school district declared it would not appeal the court's decision. The books were returned to the library shelves in 1999. The celebrated case had another consequence: Nancy Garden was so shocked by the events that she thereafter became personally involved in fighting the book ban and became an eloquent spokesperson against book censorship in general. In 2001, Garden received the Robert B. Downs Intellectual Freedom Award for her work in this area.

Further Reading

Green, Jonathon, and Nicholas J. Karolides. *Encyclopedia of Censorship, New Edition*. New York: Facts On File, 2005.

Nancy Garden official Web site. Available online: www.nancygarden. com. Accessed September 24, 2007.

"San Ramon, California." *Newsletter on Intellectual Freedom*, January 1992: 5.

Young Adult Library Services Association. *Hit List: Frequently Challenged Books for Young Adults*. Chicago: American Library Association, 1996.

About the Author of *Annie on My Mind*

Nancy Garden (1938–)

The writing of *Annie on My Mind* was a deeply personal experience for Nancy Garden, who is herself a lesbian. She was born on May 15, 1938, in Boston, Massachusetts. In high school she fell in love with the theater and later attended Columbia University's School of Dramatic Arts in New York City. She acted for four seasons in summer stock and appeared in Off Broadway productions.

Garden gradually became disillusioned by the difficulty of making a career in the theater and returned to Columbia Teachers College to get a master's degree in speech. She taught for a time, but also began to write for children. Her first work of fiction, *What Happened in Marston*, was published in 1971. After leaving New York with her partner, Sandy Scott, and settling in Massachusetts, Garden worked as a book editor in Boston and continued to write books.

Annie on My Mind (1982) is Garden's best-known and most controversial young-adult novel. Her other novels include *Lark in the Morning* (1991) and *Holly's Secret* (2000), about a girl who tries to hide the fact that she has two lesbian mothers. Garden has also written horror novels for younger readers, including *My Sister, the Vampire* (1992) and *My Brother, the Werewolf* (1995), as well as nonfiction books.

In January 2003, Garden was the recipient of the Margaret A. Edwards Award for lifetime achievement in young-adult literature. She and Scott divide their time between a small town in Massachusetts and a coastal home in Maine, where she does much of her writing.

Fools Crow (1986)
by James Welch
• • • • • • • • • • • •

What Happens in *Fools Crow*

Set in the 1870s at a critical point in the Plains Indians' battle for survival, this novel is the epic story of an eight-year-old Blackfeet Indian's journey to manhood and his role in deciding his people's fate.

White Man's Dog is insecure and undistinguished at the book's beginning. Step by step, he grows into a mature man and confident warrior. On his first warrior mission with other young men of his tribe, he steals horses from the Crows and kills his first enemy. With the help of the tribal medicine man Mik-api, the youth experiences the purging rite of the sweat lodge and learns to interpret his dreams.

Later, he marries a maiden, Red Paint, and undergoes the grueling religious rite of the Sun Dance. For his courage and stamina, he is given the name Fools Crow and begins his vision quest, disguised as a beggar. In a mythic encounter, he meets Feather Woman, who predicts a grim future for his people and their culture. "You can prepare them for the times to come," she tells Fools Crow. "If they make peace within themselves, they will live a good life in the Sand Hills. There they will go on to live as they always have. Things will not change."

He returns to his people to find Feather Woman's prophecy is coming true. Smallpox, a disease brought by the whites, kills many of the Blackfeet. In the end, Fools Crow leads his people to the reservation, where they will continue to keep their culture alive. "He knew they would survive," writes the author, "for they were the chosen ones."

Challenges and Censorship

As an historical novel about the terrible dilemma facing Native Americans in the last days of their freedom and as a mythic quest saga, *Fools Crow* has been praised and acclaimed by critics and readers alike. "[I]t was nothing anyone had read before," says Bill Bevis, author and professor emeritus at the University of Montana, on the novel's publication in 1986. "It is such a sweeping historic epic and it enlarged our country's imagination."

Although written for adults, *Fools Crow* was quickly picked up for the high school English curriculum, especially in Montana, author James Welch's home state and the setting for much of the novel. It was only after it was approved as acceptable for second-year English classes in Montana that the challenges began in that state. Most of the challenges have focused on the graphic violence in the fighting between warring tribes and between Indians and encroaching whites. Challengers have complained that the rapes, murders, and mutilations described in the book are inappropriate for middle or high school students.

Most of the challenges have been rejected, and the book has remained in classrooms. For example, in 2000 in Bozeman, Montana, the school board voted unanimously to reject a challenge and to keep the novel following a three-hour hearing. However, a 1999 challenge in Laurel, Montana, succeeded, with the local school board voting 3 to 1 to ban the book. "I just find it a surprise, and I think it's sad for the young people of Laurel," said the author regarding the decision. "They won't get to learn more about the Indian culture."

Landmark Challenge: Bad Images in Helena

Christy Dighans's first reaction when her son, a sophomore at Helena High School in Helena, Montana, complained about reading *Fools Crow* for his English class in 2007, was to send him back to the book. But when he complained again, saying he was bothered by the images in his head after reading the book, Dighans took a look herself.

"He showed me what he was referring to and I was appalled," she said. "I scanned through it one time to see if it was just in one area. When I found it was throughout the whole book, I read it all in one night."

A former military police officer, Dighans took her complaint to the school board, pointing out that she would have been happy to have her son read an alternative book, but that he wasn't aware of this option. The board countered that to be allowed a choice, her son would have had to ask for the alternative list.

"They are constantly telling us to watch out for that [violence in the media]," pressed Dighans. "We send them to school with the expectation they will provide appropriate material. This is not."

The board formed a literary review committee to look into the complaint. A short time later the committee gave its recommendation to keep *Fools Crow* on the approved reading list for sophomores at Helena High. School superintendent Bruce Messinger said that the decision of the committee was based on the high literary merit of the novel, which more than balanced, the group felt, the controversial violent acts described. He added that the district would be more diligent in the future in communicating an alternative assignment option to students and parents.

Further Reading

Cohen, Betsy. "Writer James Welch Dies at 62." *Missoulian*, August 6, 2003. Available online: www.missoulian.com/articles/2003/08/06/news/local/news02.txt. Accessed October 29, 2007.

"Helena, Montana." *Newsletter on Intellectual Freedom*, July 2007. Available online: https://members.ala.org/nif/v56n4/dateline.html. Accessed November 21, 2007.

Listoe, Alana. "School District Keeps 'Fools Crow' in Curriculum." *Helena Independent Record*, August 2, 2007. Available online: www.helenair.com/articles/2007/08/02/helena/000crow.txt. Accessed October 29, 2007.

———. "Woman Wants Book Removed from School." *Helena Independent Record*, April 13, 2007. Available online: www.helenair.com/articles/2007/04/13/helena/000book.txt. Accessed October 27, 2007.

Welch, James. "James Welch's Introduction to Our Third Catalog of Native American Literature." Ken Lopez—Bookseller Web site. Available online: www.lopezbooks.com/articles/welch.html. Accessed October 29, 2007.

About the Author of *Fools Crow*

James Welch (1940–2003)

James Welch was one of the leading Native American authors of the twentieth century. He was born on November 18, 1940, in Browning, Montana. His father was a Blackfeet and his mother belonged to the Gros Ventre tribe. He was raised on the Fort Belknap Reservation in Montana and went on to study creative writing at the University of Montana under the poet Richard Hugo. Hugo encouraged Welch to write about what he knew—contemporary Native American life. Welch's first novel, *Winter in the Blood* (1974), was a grim and critically acclaimed look at modern-day reservation life. He followed it with a collection of poetry, *Riding the Earthboy 40* (1976) and a second novel, *The Death of Jim Loney* (1979). The historical novel *Fools Crow* (1986) is perhaps his most acclaimed book; it was followed by another contemporary look at Indian life, *The Indian Lawyer* (1990). Welch's last novel, also historical, was *The Heartsong of Charging Elk* (2000). He also wrote the nonfiction book *Killing Custer: The Battle of Little Bighorn and the Fate of the Plains Indians* (1994) with Paul Stekler.

In 1997 Welch received a Lifetime Achievement Award for Literature from the Native Writers' Circle. In 2000 he was knighted in France for service to French culture through his literary works. He died at age 62 on August 4, 2003, of a heart attack while battling lung cancer.

Speaking about his poems in 1997, Welch wrote, "I was writing about a world I was born into, a world full of bones and wind—the world of my ancestors. And thirty years later, in one way or another, I am still writing about that world."

The Goats (1987)
by Brock Cole

● ● ● ● ● ● ● ● ● ● ● ● ● ●

What Happens in *The Goats*

Howie Mitchell and Laura Golden are the least popular kids at a summer camp in rural Michigan and are known as "goats," short for scapegoats. One night they become the victims of a cruel prank. A group of boy campers kidnap them and leave them marooned and naked on a deserted island across a lake from the camp.

When Howie sees approaching counselors who are looking for them, he mistakes them for the return of their tormentors and forces Laura, who can't swim, to float back to the mainland with him on a log. Afraid and angry, the two decide not to return to camp, instead hiding out until Parents' Weekend, when Laura's mother will be visiting and can take them home. During this time, the two learn about themselves and each other. They break into a cottage and find clothes to wear, hide with a different group of campers and make friends with some African Americans, and endure challenging experiences.

While all this is going on, the counselors summon Laura's mother, Maddy, a single parent who also works full time, to the camp. She learns that her daughter and Howie are missing. As Maddy discovers more details of what happened, she becomes upset with the camp and refuses to cooperate with the counselors. In the process, she becomes a more caring parent.

As they make their way back to camp and to Maddy, the two teens form a meaningful friendship, growing and maturing from whiny nerds into confident and responsible young people. Before they can reach Maddy, however, a sheriff's deputy apprehends them. They manage to escape and take his car.

In the book's closing pages, they finally reach Maddy and their strange adventure comes to an end. "Suddenly he [Howie] was very sure that everything was going to be all right," the author writes. "He wasn't a fool. He knew that there would be arguments and long-distance phone calls, and parents and camp counselors and policemen talking over their head about things he didn't understand. He would want to crawl in a hole, and she would cry. It didn't matter. They would think of something. They could look at each other now and smile."

Challenges and Censorship

Brock Cole's sensitive story about two misfits who find themselves in trying circumstances was highly praised upon its publication in 1987. A reviewer for *School Library Journal* called it "a strong, well-balanced story of modern day survival." *Kirkus Review* said it was "a sensitive portrayal . . . a tale of underdogs triumphant," while *Horn Book* hailed it as a "significant addition to the body of children's literature." Betsy Hearne, editor of the *Bulletin of the Center for Children's Books*, called *The Goats* "one of the most important books of the decade."

However, strong language, adult situations, and the violence of certain scenes (such as the marooning) have drawn many challenges in schools and school libraries. There is also the fact that Howie and Laura, the two central characters, commit a number of crimes, including stealing change from cars, breaking and entering people's homes, and stealing the car of the deputy who arrests them. While they do intend to pay back everyone they have stolen from—and even keep a running tab of what they owe—some challengers did not find this sufficient. *The Goats* ranked thirtieth in the American Library Association's "100 Most Frequently Challenged Books of 1990–2000."

Despite the numerous challenges, the novel continues to be popular with young readers. Recently an anniversary edition was released with Cole's original cover art.

Landmark Challenge:
A Hot Time in Terre Haute

Of the some 80 concerned citizen who attended the book review committee meeting at the Thornton Center gym in Terre Haute, Indiana, on November 5, 1997, only four would be allowed to speak their mind about Brock Cole's novel *The Goat*. This could not have pleased the other 75, most of whom supported the book's use in local schools. They included an author, a bookstore owner, and several college professors.

The four who did get to speak represented 53 residents who had signed a petition to ban the book from all district classrooms and all recommended reading lists for being morally offensive. "This is not about getting rid of a book," insisted Beverly Thompson, one of the four who spoke. She explained it was about parents' rights to see that school reading materials reflected their moral values. Another speaker, Robin Plank, was willing to compromise with the book's defenders. She suggested that it could stay in classrooms, but that its use be restricted by means of a new rating system for all classroom materials.

After 50 minutes, the eight-member committee brought the public meeting to a close. Later, the committee voted to reject the challenge and declared *The Goats* appropriate for reading by both middle and high school students. The book's opponents immediately appealed the decision to the school board. The issue, however, was a complicated one. The district had no formal policy in place to bring the school board into the decision-making process.

At a school board meeting in November, defenders of the book got their chance to speak publicly to board members. In an editorial on November 12, the *Terre Haute Tribune-Star* urged the school board "to deal with the book-banning issue quickly and aggressively. The community is tuned into the debate and an expeditious hearing and ruling would be in the corporation's best interests."

The issue apparently was still undecided in January 1998. In a letter to the editor of the *Tribune-Star*, a longtime resident expressed frustration at the continuing debate over the book challenge. He complained of "suppression of testimony, awkwardly timed public hearing, condescending obfuscation and name-calling. . . . The community will be better off with reduced tension between the public and its education when all the peaceable discussion is made public."

Further Reading

Letter to the Editor from Bruce Spidel. *Terre Haute Tribune-Star*, January 11, 1998.
"Now Is the Board's Turn." *Terre Haute Tribune-Star*, November 12, 1997.

"Terre Haute, Indiana." *Newsletter on Intellectual Freedom*, January 1998: 11; March 1998: 55.

About the Author of *The Goats*

Brock Cole (1938–)

Brock Cole was born on May 29, 1938, in Charlotte, Michigan. His family moved frequently during his childhood, something he didn't mind. "I had a deep and intimate acquaintance with woodlots, creeks, lakes, back streets, and alleys all over the Midwest," he later wrote. He attended Kenyon College in Ohio, majoring in English. After graduating, he earned a doctorate in philosophy from the University of Minnesota and taught philosophy for several years at the University of Wisconsin. He became a full-time writer in 1975.

A talented illustrator, Cole's first published works were humorous picture books for children, which he both wrote and illustrated. They included *The King at the Door* (1979), *Nothing But a Pig* (1981), and *The Giant's Toe* (1986), a clever parody of the story "Jack and the Beanstalk."

The Goats (1987) was his first, and remains his most popular, young-adult (YA) novel to date. His other YA novels include *Celine* (1989) and *The Facts Speak for Themselves* (1997).

Brock Cole lives in Buffalo, New York, with his wife, Susan, who teaches at the State University of New York (SUNY) at Buffalo. They travel frequently outside the United States and have spent time in Germany, Greece, and Turkey. "There's something about sitting down to work at a rickety table in a strange city that clears the head," Cole says. "It's the best thing for a writer, or for this one, anyway."

Fallen Angels (1988)
by Walter Dean Myers
• • • • • • • • • • • • •

What Happens in *Fallen Angels*

Richard Perry, a 17-year-old black senior graduating from high school in New York City, doesn't know what to do with his life. He decides to join the Army and is sent to basic training and then to Vietnam, where a war is raging.

The men in his unit are a cross section of humanity. They include Peewee, who never loses his sense of humor; Lobel, who sees every incident of war as part of an ongoing movie; and Monaco, who is Italian American. Stationed in Chu Lai, Vietnam, the soldiers' mission is to fight the enemy, the Vietcong, and root out local villagers who support them. Here death comes swiftly and life is cheap. When Jenkins, a member of Perry's unit, dies from a land-mine explosion, Perry is traumatized by the senselessness of it. Any illusions he had that the war would soon be over are dashed by the empty promises of politicians and probing reporters who ask all the wrong questions.

After being wounded twice, Perry finally receives the good news that he is going home. The war for him will be over, but it has robbed Perry of his innocence. For better or worse, he is a different person.

Challenges and Censorship

Fallen Angels, a harrowing look at the Vietnam War through the eyes of a 17-year-old African-American soldier, remains one of the few young-adult novels that deals with this still controversial conflict. When first published in 1986, the novel was praised by critics for its realism and its soldier's-eye view of a war few people in America fully understood. Walter Dean Myers himself was a soldier in Vietnam and his personal experience brings weight and reality to the story. *Fallen Angels* was the recipient of the Coretta Scott King Award in 1989 and the Margaret A. Edwards Award in 1994.

While the book makes no direct judgment on the war, its strong language and explicit violence have been responsible for most of the challenges made against it. *Fallen Angels* ranks twenty-fourth on the American Library Association's "100 Most Frequently Challenged Books of 1990–2000." It also made the ALA's top ten lists for most frequently challenged books in 1999, 2000, and 2001.

Even some parents and administrators who appreciate the realism Myers put into his book remain critical of it. "I think the language portrays what went on in Vietnam very accurately," admitted a trustee in the Livonia, Michigan, school district in 1999. "But I don't think we should require a fourteen-year-old to read it."

Landmark Challenge: "A Small Step in the Right Direction"

A simple challenge by a parent in the Blue Valley School District in Overland Park, Kansas, in 2003, was the beginning of an influential and outspoken parents' organization. The book in question was *This Boy's Life*, a memoir by Tobias Wolff then used in the high school communications arts classes. The challenge made by parent Janet Harmon and her husband was turned down by the Blue Valley school board. But the Harmons' advocacy of greater parental involvement in the choosing of curriculum materials had its impact.

A short time later, the board made a special review of all titles used in the high school communications arts classes. While the review was going on, Janet Harmon got organized. In 2004 she founded, with other concerned parents, Citizens for Literary Standards in Schools, more popularly known as ClassKC. Five members of the group collected 500 signatures on a petition calling for the removal of 14 books from the communications arts class required reading list. The books included *This Boy's Life* and *Fallen Angels*, which the group claimed had inappropriate content.

The petition was rejected by the school board, but on August 8, 2005, the board removed the two novels and three other books from the fall curriculum. The special review committee that recommended the action said the decision was based not on improper content, but the books' failure to meet new curriculum requirements. *Fallen Angels* was replaced by another novel about the Vietnam War—*Going After Cacciato*, by Tim O'Brien. "It's a small step in the right direction," said Harmon, "and we hope that there will be many more steps like this made."

Her hopes were soon fulfilled. The yearlong review by the school board led to a number of other changes in curriculum selection. New rationales, or statements, were developed and put on a Web site that gave a plot summary and other information about each book on the reading list. The most controversial part of the rationales was a feature called "A Note on the Text" that warned parents about any sensitive or objectionable material in each book.

"This is huge," said Harmon. "This is great, especially if they are publicized online. This was our goal from the beginning, just to let parents know what their children are reading."

Even those who opposed ClassKC expressed little doubt about the school board's actions. "I guess I have to say if they [the books] were truly taken off because they no longer fit the curriculum, that's their prerogative," said Blue Valley North High School junior Kerry McGuire, who organized a counterpetition supporting the books.

In 2004 ClassKC recruited Gregg Motley, former Kansas City director of the National Coalition for the Protection of Children and Families. Motley has been moving the organization to become aligned with other similar groups across the country in order to increase its clout.

While other districts have adopted ClassKC's tactics, the group itself has suffered setbacks recently. Five books survived its 2006 book challenges and the Blue Valley school board has consistently rebuffed its efforts. "We've made some progress as far as talking to parents and making parents aware," said ClassKC spokesperson Heidi Harper. "And the unfortunate thing is, I don't know how much progress we've made with the district."

Further Reading

"Author Profile: Walter Dean Myers." Teenreads.com. Available online: www.teenreads.com/authors/au-myers-walterdean.asp. Accessed July 12, 2007.

Green, Jonathon, and Nicholas J. Karolides. *Encyclopedia of Censorship, New Edition.* New York: Facts On File, 2005.

Kendall, Justin. "Meet the Parent." Pitch, June 15, 2006. Available online: www.pitch.com/2006-06-15/news/meet-the-parent. Accessed October 1, 2007.

"Overland Park, Kansas." *Newsletter on Intellectual Freedom,* November 2005. Available online: https://members.ala.org/nif/v54n6/dateline. html. Accessed November 21, 2007.

Young Adult Library Services Association. *Hit List: Frequently Challenged Books for Young Adults.* Chicago: American Library Association, 1996

About the Author of *Fallen Angels*

Walter Dean Myers (1937–   )

Walter Dean Myers is one of the best-known African-American authors of books for young adults. Much of his work focuses on the mean streets of New York's Harlem, where he grew up, and the challenges faced by black youths struggling to find meaning and identity in their lives.

He was born on August 12, 1937, in Martinsburg, West Virginia. His mother died when he was three and his father, unable to provide for him, gave him up to a foster family, the Deans, in Harlem. Walter was loved and nurtured by his foster parents and took their name as part of his own.

Although an avid reader and a good writer, young Walter was plagued by speech problems that made it difficult to make himself understood. In frustration, he dropped out of high school and joined the Army. He served in Vietnam during the Vietnam War, an experience he vividly recreated in his novel *Fallen Angels* (1988). After being discharged, he took courses in writing at the City College of the City University of New York (CUNY) and later attended Empire State College. He married in 1960 and had two children, but the marriage ended in divorce. During these lean years he worked in the post office while writing at night. Eventually he started getting his work published in periodicals such as the *National Enquirer.* He also wrote ad copy for cemeteries.

In 1969, Myers entered a manuscript in a competition held by the Council on Interracial Books for Children. His winning entry became his first published book, *Where Does the Day Go?* His first young-adult novel, *Fast Sam, Cool Clyde, and Stuff*, appeared in 1975. Among his other critically acclaimed novels are *The Glory Field* (1994); *Monster* (1999), winner of the Michael L. Printz Award for excellence in young-adult literature; and *Shooter* (2005), about a school shooting. Myers has also written books of nonfiction (*A Place Called Heartbreak: A Story of Vietnam*, 1993) and biographies (*Malcolm X: A Fire Burning Brightly*, 2000).

Walter Dean Myers lives with his second wife in Jersey City, New Jersey. "Ultimately, what I want to do with my writing is to make connections," he has said, "to touch the lives of my characters and, through them, those of my readers."

The Drowning of Stephan Jones (1991)
by Bette Greene

What Happens in *The Drowning of Stephan Jones*

Carla Wayland is madly in love with Andy Harris and is willing to overlook his faults—including his prejudices against people who are different, especially gay people. The small town of Rachetville, Arkansas, where they live, nurtures this kind of prejudice. That's why when Andy and his friends run into Frank and Stephan, a gay couple who have just moved to the area, their aggressive behavior is tolerated if not condoned.

When Carla attends Christmas services at Andy's church, even Reverend Wheelwright, the pastor, shows his hatred for homosexuality in an impassioned sermon. Carla grows uneasy as the harassment against the gay men intensifies. Perhaps she is more like her nonconformist mother than she would care to admit. Judith Wayland is the town's librarian and an outspoken defender of intellectual freedom.

Frank and Stephan open an antique shop in the area, but Andy and his friends are determined to drive them out of the community. When they encounter Stephan in a pizza parlor, they chase him and burn his face with hot pizza. Threatening telephone calls and letters follow. Seeking help from the growing harassment, Frank and Stephan turn to Reverend Wheelwright, but he offers them no sympathy or assistance.

Carla looks forward to the night of the high school prom as the fulfillment of all her dreams. But Andy turns it into a nightmare for her. He and two friends pursue Stephan to a river and hurl him into it. As Carla watches, Stephan drowns, and the threesome is later arrested for his death. Andy claims it was Stephan's unwelcome advances that drove him to the attack, and he and the others get off with suspended sentences and probation. Only at the novel's end does the truth come out. Frank confronts Andy during his celebration party after the verdict and displays the love letters that Andy wrote to Stephan. It was Stephan's rejection that fueled Andy's anger all along. Soon after, Carla and her mother move away from Rachetville and its terrible memories.

Challenges and Censorship

Bette Greene wrote *The Drowning of Stephan Jones* out of a deep conviction that prejudice and hatred of outsiders is wrong. "I am straight and have been married to the same man for thirty-four years," she said in a 1994 interview, "but I don't understand brutalizing somebody because they are physically attracted to people in ways that I may not be."

Greene based her novel on a real-life case. She did extensive research into hate crimes against gay people, interviewing about 485 people in eight states. The people she interviewed included victims, victimizers, and others associated with these crimes. "I talked to everyone who was available—their [the victimizers'] teachers, their Uncle Joe, their pastors, their coaches," she said. "I tried to find out where does the hate come from? Not all the boys were religious but they all had been affected by religion. They knew it was OK to do violence to gay people because they thought it said so in the Bible."

One of the main villains of *The Drowning of Stephan Jones* is the church pastor, Reverend Wheelwright, and this is no accident. "A great amount of [homophobia in America] is coming from fundamental Christianity. . . . Nobody can be more in error than when they insist that they, and they alone, speak for God."

Greene's outspoken criticism of certain conservative religious groups has increased the number of challenges to her novel, which ranked ninety-fourth on the American Library Association's "100 Most Frequently Challenged Books of 1990–2000." It has also led to a more personal rejection. In April 2000 Greene was scheduled to talk at Harding University, a Church of Christ school of higher learning in Searcy, Arkansas, when the invitation was abruptly withdrawn. A spokesperson from Harding said that the engagement had never been formally set. Greene has suggested the cancellation was related to the content of *The Drowning of Stephan Jones.*

Landmark Challenge:
The Firing of Penny Culliton

Teacher Penny Culliton thought she was acting appropriately, and with the approval of her school superintendent and principal, when she purchased a number of classroom books depicting gay and lesbian life for her eleventh- and twelfth-grade students at Mascenic Regional High School in New Ipswich, New Hampshire. The books included the novels *The Drowning of Stephan Jones*, E. M. Forster's *Maurice*, and May Sarton's *The Education of Harriet Hatfield.*

But when a local newspaper story said that she was teaching a gay and lesbian unit in her classes while working with a gay and lesbian support group for young people, school officials became concerned. They told Culliton not to distribute the books to her students. When she refused, the school board dismissed her in September 1995, accusing her of "willful insubordination." Their decision said: "Ms. Culliton intentionally engaged students, during class time, in a tacit, if not overt, protest of the principal's proper directive that she collect the books from students."

Penny Culliton did not accept the dismissal quietly. She fought the decision and got the support of the largest teachers' union in New Hampshire. "None of this has anything to do with my teaching," she countered. "It has to do with intolerance and other people's insecurities when a group they are used to looking at as being inferior to themselves asks to be regarded on an equal plane. All along I've tried to do what's best for my students."

Many of her students stood by her. On September 27, about 80 students walked out of class and conducted a demonstration on school grounds. Some carried a large banner that read: "Support Miss Culliton. Fight Censorship." To alleviate the tense situation, school officials told the demonstrators that if they returned to class they would not be reprimanded and that a discussion about Culliton's dismissal would take place at a later date. Half the students returned to class; the other half continued to demonstrate. Parent Cindy Ouellette received a call from school officials asking her to pick up her son, who was demonstrating. Ouellette came to school with her other son and joined the demonstrators. Marissa Steinberg's mother came and through tears told her daughter, "I'm proud of you for doing this."

Another parent present was New Ipswich Police Chief Malboeuf. His daughter Lori was one of the demonstration's organizers. "They have beliefs, and they're young adults and they should be able to express them," Chief Malbouef told reporters at the scene. School officials suspended the remaining demonstrators for a day. For Lori Malboeuf, it was worth the punishment. "At least we made our opinions known that we're not happy with the school board," she said.

Penny Culliton was not immediately reinstated, but parents, students, and fellow teachers continued to plead her cause. Arbitrators from the teachers' union worked out a compromise. Her dismissal was reduced to a one-year suspension and was upheld by the state's Public Employee Labor Relations Board. Culliton was formally reinstated by the school board in the fall of 1996. "If it were any other subject matter, Penny would not have been dismissed," said Dennis Murphy, a lobbyist for the National Educators' Association (NEA).

Landmark Challenge:
Risk of Removal in Barron, Wisconsin

When parent Karen Williams asked Barron High School librarian Irene Cooley for a list of books dealing with "alternative lifestyles" in March 1998, Cooley was most obliging. She had second thoughts, however, when, one by one, the 14 books she directed Williams to were challenged as inappropriate for students in Barron, Wisconsin. "She has been working off that list pretty much throughout this," Cooley said.

The first books Williams challenged were the novels *The Drowning of Stephan Jones* and Francesca Lia Block's *Baby Be-Bop* and the nonfiction books *When Someone You Know Is Gay*, by Susan and Daniel Cohen, and *Two Teenagers in Twenty*, by Ann Heron. All four dealt with issues of gay and lesbian life. The challenges were brought before the district's Book Reconsideration Committee. After due deliberations, the committee recommended that the books remain on high school library shelves. But in September 1998, the Barron District school board rejected the recommendation and voted 7 to 2 to remove all four books.

In the meantime, Williams worked down her list and challenged four more books with gay themes, including the novel *Jack*, by A. M. Homes. "What troubles me," said Pat Solheid, a member of the Book Reconsideration Committee, "is that I think this puts vast amounts of literature at risk of removal."

The board met again on December 21, 1998, to reconsider the removal of the first four books. Some 60 residents attended the meeting; a number of them spoke out for or against the books. "Censorship is at the heart of the matter," said Kathy Duerr, a middle-school staff worker. "As educators, it is our duty to introduce students to a variety of ideas and beliefs." But for Noel Hargis, most students were not mature enough to deal with the subject matter. "As a school board you have to think of the weakest students, not the strongest," he said.

When it came time to vote, the board reaffirmed the removal of the two novels, but agreed to keep the nonfiction books on the library shelves until updated books with more accurate information could be found. "If we are going to provide students with medical information [such as on AIDS], we have a duty to see it is accurate," said district superintendent Vita Sherry.

Chris Ahmuty, executive director of American Civil Liberties Union (ACLU) of Wisconsin, was disturbed by the vote and vowed to fight the decision. "We are chagrined that the board is harming its students, both straight and lesbian or gay," said Ahmuty. "It is harming its lesbian and gay students by sending them a terrible message of exclusion and intolerance. The board may not establish a narrow orthodoxy in its library because it is offended by lesbian or gay subject matter."

On February 16, 1999, the ACLU filed a suit against the district on behalf of several students and their parents in U.S. District Court in Madison. District officials prepared their defense against the suit, but to avoid further litigation, they agreed to return the books to the library while the case was ongoing.

"The action that the board took, that nobody will read these certain books, is wrong," said Maureen Wigchers, one of the parent plaintiffs and a custodian in the school system. "Those of us willing to put our names on this are taking a risk, but it's something we feel very strongly about."

Further Reading

Alvine, Lynne. "Understanding Adolescent Homophobia: An Interview with Bette Greene." *The ALAN Review*, winter 1994. Available online: http://scholar.lib.vt.edu/ejournals/ALAN/winter94/Alvine.html. Accessed September 26, 2007.

"Barron, Wisconsin." *Newsletter on Intellectual Freedom*, January 1999: 9; March 1999: 37; May 1999: 68.

Foerstel, Herbert N. *Banned in the U.S.A.: A Reference Guide to Book Censorship in Schools and Public Libraries.* Westport, Conn.: Greenwood Press, 2002.

"Mascenic, New Hampshire." *Newsletter on Intellectual Freedom*, January 1997: 27.

"New Ipswich, New Hampshire." *Newsletter on Intellectual Freedom*, January 1996: 15.

Young Adult Library Services Association. *Hit List: Frequently Challenged Books for Young Adults.* Chicago: American Library Association, 1996.

About the Author of *The Drowning of Stephan Jones*

Bette Greene (1934–   )

See biography in *Summer of My German Soldier* entry.

Baseball Saved Us (1993)
by Ken Mochizuki

• • • • • • • • • • • • • •

What Happens in *Baseball Saved Us*

In 1942, Shorty and his family, along with thousands of other Japanese Americans, are removed from their homes by the United States government and placed in internment camps in remote areas. This indignity is in reaction to the Japanese attack on Pearl Harbor, although nearly all Japanese Americans at the time were loyal U.S. citizens.

Unable to work or do much of anything in the internment camps, the people grow restless. Shorty's father comes up with the idea of playing baseball. Along with other men, he creates a baseball field. The women make baseball uniform out of mattress ticking. Soon, Shorty is playing baseball regularly with the other boys. His short stature and lack of athletic skill make Shorty a weak player at first. Through determination and practice, however, Shorty overcomes these impediments to become a good baseball player. During one game, he focuses his anger and frustration on a guard watching over them, and hits a home run out of the ballpark. The guard reacts with a smile and a wave, surprising Shorty.

When the war ends and Shorty and his family are released from the camp, they return to their lives in Seattle, Washington. Shorty becomes a member of his school baseball team, but again must prove himself to put a stop to the racial slurs and prejudice.

Challenges and Censorship

The subject matter of *Baseball Saved Us*, Ken Mochizuki's first book for children, was a natural for the author. His Japanese-American parents were sent to an internment camp in Idaho from their home in Seattle, Washington, in 1942, along with thousands of other Japanese Americans. The American government, reeling from the surprise attack by the Japanese on Pearl Harbor in December 1941, wanted to keep close watch over all Japanese in this country, despite the fact that the vast majority of them were loyal Americans. Most of the interned Japanese Americans and their families remained in these camps through the end of World War II three years later. This dark chapter in American history has only been widely publicized relatively recently. Ken Mochizuki's book, published in 1993, was one of the first children's books to be written on the subject.

The book was well reviewed and has become a staple in school and public libraries. Most readers have seen the book as a strong argument against prejudice and racism. Mochizuki is an outspoken opponent to all forms of prejudice and travels widely, speaking to students about his book and its message. He points out that he is hardly the stereotype of a Japanese-American male. He is not a computer nerd, wasn't very good at math in school, and has little interest in the martial arts.

There have been relatively few challenges to *Baseball Saved Us*. The one described here was based on the use of a racial slur.

Landmark Challenge: A Singular Slur in New Milford

Baseball Saved Us would have been an acceptable book for elementary school students according to Peter and Wendy O'Brien, except for one unfortunate word. The word was "Jap," spoken by a child to another child, and it led the O'Briens, parents of a second grader in New Milford, Connecticut, to challenge the book's use in elementary schools.

"I was kind of shocked," said Peter O'Brien, when presenting his complaint to assistant superintendent Thomas Mulvihill and Committee on Learning chairman William McLachlan. "I don't think it is necessary to bring up a racial slur in second grade."

In an earlier letter to Mulvihill, O'Brien wrote, "Any ethnic slur should not be introduced at the elementary level, period. There is simply no need for it." The letter led Mulvihill to create a citizens' request form for reconsideration of a book already on an approved reading list. It was the first form of its kind in the district.

In reaction to the challenge, Irene Kwidzinski, librarian at the Northville School, defended the book, calling it "a learning opportunity." According to Kwidzinski, "Students learn about tolerance and diversity and how not to repeat history. That's the value of books like that. You want them to think critically. It is a book of its time. It reflects what society thought at that time." She did acknowledge that for young students, the reading and discussion of the book had to be handled "with sensitivity and guidance." She recommended reading be followed by discussion with teachers or parents of how words and language can hurt individuals.

Further Reading

"Meet Authors & Illustrators: Ken Mochizuki." Children's Literature Comprehensive Database Web site. Available online: www.childrenslit.com/ childrenslit/mai_mochizuki_ken.html. Accessed October 30, 2007.

"New Milford, Connecticut." *Newsletter on Intellectual Freedom*, July 2006: 183–184. Available online: https://members.ala.org/nif/v55n4/ dateline.html.

About the Author of *Baseball Saved Us*

Ken Mochizuki (1954–)

A prominent Japanese-American author for young readers, Ken Mochizuki scored a home run with his first book, *Baseball Saved Us*, in 1993. He was born on May 22, 1954, in Seattle, Washington. His Japanese-American family had come to America close to a century earlier. After graduating from the University of Washington, where he majored in communications, Mochizuki moved to Los Angeles, California, where he pursued a career in acting. He appeared on several television series, including an episode of the comedy-drama *M*A*S*H*. After five years, he returned to Seattle and got a job as a staff reporter and editor for a newspaper.

Mochizuki's first children's book, *Baseball Saved Us*, with illustrations by Dom Lee, appeared to great acclaim in 1993. He has written two other picture books about the Japanese-American experience: *Heroes* (1997) deals with Korean War veterans, while *Passage to Freedom: The Sugihara Story* (2003) is a biography of the Japanese consul Hiroki Sugihara, who saved the lives the hundreds of European Jews from the Nazi death camps in World War II. In

2002, Mochizuki published his first young-adult novel, *Beacon Hill Boys*, a semi-autobiographical book about his high school years in a multiethnic school.

When not writing, Ken Mochizuki spends much of his time traveling the country speaking to schoolchildren and others about racial prejudice.

The Buffalo Tree (1997)
by Adam Rapp

• • • • • • • • • • • • •

What Happens in *The Buffalo Tree*

Thirteen-year-old Sura, narrator of this harrowing novel, is in Hamstock, a juvenile detention center, facing a six-month sentence for stealing car hood ornaments. "The Stock," as it is called by its inmates, is a dangerous place where a prisoner is at the mercy of the sadistic games played by the other inmates and the center's authorities. Sura makes friends with Coly Jo, his cellmate, and the two make plans to escape. But when Coly Jo is taunted by the Stock's worst bullies, he begins a downward spiral that Sura is helpless to save him from.

Sura gets a new cellmate, nicknamed Long Neck, a threatening figure who steals the escape plans. With courage and a growing maturity, Sura manages to survive his sentence and is released. But he will never forget the experience. "You get that old feeling back up in your bones just for a second," he says near the book's end. "You get that feeling that the night's got something up its sleeve for you. Even if it's during the day you get that feeling."

Challenges and Censorship

The Buffalo Tree, published in 1997, cemented Rapp's reputation as a young-adult writer who, like Chris Lynch and Robert Cormier, is not afraid to tackle the darkest and most controversial subjects. While violence permeates the world that Rapp writes about, he feels he uses it responsibly in his fiction and plays. "I think violence can become gratuitous when it's not serving the story," he said in a 2000 interview. "I try and steer clear of this as much as possible. In general

I feel that my responsibility as an artist is to tell the truth, and it's as simple as that."

Given the controversial nature of *The Buffalo Tree* and its no-holds-barred depiction of life in a male juvenile detention center, it is surprising that only one major challenge has surfaced against the book.

Landmark Challenge: An Argument over Values in Muhlenberg

The Buffalo Tree had been on the eleventh-grade reading list for five years at Muhlenberg High School in Muhlenberg, Pennsylvania. But that counted for little when, on an evening in April 2005, 16-year-old Brittany Hunsicker stood up at a meeting of the local school board, brandishing a copy of the novel she had been instructed to read in English class.

"How would you like if your son and daughter had to read this?" she asked, and then commenced reading an excerpt from the novel that graphically depicted the sexual arousal of a teenager taking a communal shower in a junior detention center. When stopped by stunned board members, Hunsicker said, "I am in the eleventh grade. I had to read this junk."

Within an hour, the board voted unanimously to ban *The Buffalo Tree* from the school's curriculum. The next morning, all copies of the novel were collected by administrators and placed in a vault in the principal's office. Students and teachers were appalled by the board's swift decision and subsequent actions. They cried out for the book's reinstatement. Superintendent of schools Joseph Yarworth agreed that the board had made a rush to judgment. He ordered the copies of the book returned to classrooms, where those students who wished to read the novel could.

On the growing conflict over the book, Yarworth noted, "We're absolutely middle-American. And we're having an argument over values." The argument spilled over into the *Reading Eagle*, the local newspaper, where letters both for and against *The Buffalo Tree* and book banning in general soon started to appear.

On May 4, the school board convened to reconsider its decision with 200 residents present. After making a public apology for the board's quick actions, board president Mark Nelson opened the floor to residents. Two hours of lively debate followed. In sharp contrast to junior Brittany Hunsicker, senior Mary Isamoyer was passionate in her defense of the book. "Do not insult our intelligence by keeping that book from us," she told the board. "This is not about a child's opinion," countered Tammy Hahn, a parent of four. "This is about parents." After everyone had the opportunity to speak, the board postponed the decision for another week.

On May 11 the board met again. In a lengthy discussion, Miss Hunsicker was criticized for refusing to read the book, without making the reasons for her objection to the novel clear to her teacher. English teacher Stacia Richmond made a strong stand for her department's reasons for including the book. "No one is more critical of literature than English teachers," she said. "Do you really think we as educators choose literature in terms of its titillation? Do you not realize we are battling the same immorality you are?"

In an informal poll the board voted 5 to 3 to reverse its earlier decision. However, Nelson entertained a suggestion from Hahn of a rating system for all school reading materials.

A week later, the board met again. It rejected the new policy for challenges put forth by the English department and considered Hahn's rating system. It suggested that parents be sent students' reading lists along with plot summaries and an indication of content that might be considered objectionable. The English department, speaking through chairman Michael Anthony, strenuously objected to the rating system, stating it would only lead to more challenges and more potential banning. Dr. Yarworth worked for a compromise between the two groups, but Anthony was not optimistic. "*The Buffalo Tree* isn't coming back anytime soon," he said.

Further Reading

Angel, Ann. "The Bad Boys of YA: Chris Lynch and Adam Rapp." *The ALAN Review*, fall 2000. Available online: http://scholar.lib.vt.edu/ejournals/ALAN/v28n1/angel.html. Accessed August 13, 2007.

"Muhlenberg, Pennsylvania." *Newsletter on Intellectual Freedom*, July 2005. Available online: https://members.ala.org/nif/v54n4/dateline.html. Accessed November 21, 2007.

Weber, Bruce. "A Town's Struggle in the Culture War." *New York Times*, June 2, 2005: E1. Available online: www.nytimes.com/2005/06/02/books/02ban.html.

About the Author of *The Buffalo Tree*

Adam Rapp (1968–   )

Adam Rapp is a versatile writer who has forged a successful career as a novelist, playwright, screenwriter, and filmmaker. He was born on June 15, 1968, in Chicago, Illinois, one of three children. His parents divorced when he was five and Adam was raised by his mother. After attending Clarke College in Iowa, he studied playwriting at the Juilliard School in New York City.

His first novel for young adults, *Missing the Piano*, was published in 1994 and was named a Best Book for Young Adults and Best Book for Reluctant Readers by the American Library Association the following year. His other novels include *The Buffalo Tree* (1997); *Little Chicago* (1998), about the sexual abuse of a young boy; *The Copper Elephant* (1999), a grim futuristic tale; and *The Year of Endless Sorrows* (2006), the story of a young Midwesterner's adventures at a New York publishing house.

Rapp is an Obie Award–winning playwright and director. A number of his plays have been performed Off and Off-Off Broadway in New York City. He is currently the playwright-in-residence at the Edge Theater Company in Manhattan. Rapp directed his first film, *Winter Passing*, starring Will Ferrell, in 2005.

"I hope that they [his readers] feel they have spent time with somebody special," Rapp said in an interview. "And that they might close the book and want to know what happens to the protagonist. Like the way one perhaps feels when a good friend moves away. A yearning to know more."

Nappy Hair (1997)
by Carolivia Herron

What Happens in *Nappy Hair*

This delightful children's picture book is the story of Brenda, a young African-American girl with supposedly the nappiest hair in the world. The story is told by Brenda's Uncle Mordecai, who compares combing Brenda's hair to scrunching across a hot desert or crunching through snow. Mordecai's story is interrupted throughout by the comments of other family members, in the style of a black church meeting. Mordecai's story of Brenda's nappy hair is, by the book's end, a celebration of black pride and her African heritage. As he declares, "One nap of her hair is the only perfect circle in nature."

Challenges and Censorship

Carolivia Herron didn't set out to be a children's book author; it happened by accident. She was teaching English at California State University at Chico and working on her first novel when she read passages from the work in progress at the Anacostia Museum and Center for African American History and Culture in Washington, D.C. The audience was particularly impressed by a vignette in the novel about nappy hair.

"I encouraged her to get it published as a children's book," said museum educator Joanna Banks. "I thought it would be something for African-American children to celebrate." Herron took Banks's advice. "I wrote it delighting in nappy hair," she said. "I love my own nappy hair and the stories my uncle used to tell me about it. It was a celebration, and I had no idea it would be political. I am a '60s person and thought we had already dealt with this problem of being ashamed of our hair."

The reviews were enthusiastic for this children's book, with its wonderful illustrations by Joe Cepeda, and it has sold more than 300,000 copies to date. Yet some readers, especially in the black community, took the book as racist in attitude. The one major challenge in 1998 was so public, it largely cleared the air about the book, and few further challenges in schools have been reported.

Landmark Challenge: Rush to Judgment in Bushwick

November 23, 1997, is a day that Ruth Sherman, an elementary teacher at P.S. 75 in Bushwick, Brooklyn, New York, will never forget. When she walked out of her classroom that morning to attend a meeting, little did she know that she would never return to it.

When Sherman, then an idealistic 27-year-old, told her friends in middle-class Long Island that she would be teaching in Bushwick, a tough inner-city neighborhood, they were surprised. "I chose that school because I wanted the neighborhood," she told them. "I was going to turn things around, really make a difference."

One way she hoped to do this was by presenting books that her mostly black and Latino third-grade class could relate to. One of these was *Nappy Hair*, by Carolivia Herron. Her students responded enthusiastically to this picture book about a little black girl with kinky or nappy hair.

"These were children who hated reading, that never opened a book and had difficulty reading," she later said. "I'm talking about comprehension and even word recognition. Some of them couldn't read the word 'the' and for them to be enthusiastic and excited about reading, that was really something." They were so enthusiastic that they begged Sherman to give them copies of the book to read on their own. She readily obliged and ran off photocopies and distributed them to students.

Then, in early November, a parent of one of her students came across the photocopied pages in her daughter's school folder. The title and illustrations incensed her. She immediately misinterpreted the entire book as a racial slur against African-American children. A short time later the parent came into Sherman's classroom waving the pages of the book in front of her. "[She] said she was surprised she didn't see a white [Ku Klux Klan] hat on my desk," Sherman later said. Rejecting Sherman's explanations, the parent ran off more copies of the pages and put them into the mailboxes of other parents and community residents, with a note about this racist literature being taught to their children by a "white teacher."

The note and pages had the desired effect. On November 23, the Monday before Thanksgiving break, a meeting was held in the school auditorium. It was supposed to be about the hiring of a new assistant principal, but the angry parents who attended had only one issue on their minds—*Nappy Hair* and the white teacher who had the nerve to teach it to their children. Principal Felicita Santiago summoned Sherman to the meeting, telling her she would only be gone from her classroom for 10 minutes. In fact, she would never step into the room or see her students again.

As Sherman approached the auditorium she could hear angry voices in the air. Something, she realized, was very wrong. She stopped off in the principal's office and phoned her fiancé. "I think something bad is happening," she told him. "Please come get me."

Her worst expectations were soon fulfilled. The scene in the auditorium was one of total chaos. It got worse when Sherman entered the room. "They started getting in my face, asking me who I thought I was reading that book, calling me a cracker," recalled Sherman. "Nobody would let me, or the principal, or the librarian . . . talk."

"It was an ambush," said Principal Santiago. "They turned into a lynch mob." Fearing for Sherman's safety, Santiago and a security guard hustled her out of the auditorium. District superintendent Felix Vazquez, also present, told her to go home. "He told me he heard people saying they wanted to do me bodily harm," said Sherman. "And that was it. I never saw my students again."

The next day Vazquez reassigned Sherman to desk work at district headquarters, rather than risk having her return to the school. Physical threats had been made, although the teacher decided not to press any charges. Rather than support her, however, several school officials blamed her for not clearing the teaching of the book with her principal.

"We're not censoring the book," declared local school board president Dennis Herring, who is African American. "We're not saying it should be banned. . . . The superintendent wants to make sure that staff review material with the principal."

A second parent meeting held later that same day was in sharp contrast to the first. Tempers had cooled. Some parents had read the entire book and realized that it was a celebration of black heritage and hair—not a denigration of it. Others admitted that their response might have been very different if the teacher presenting the book, like the author, had been black.

The chancellor of New York City schools, Rudy Crew, wrote a personal letter to Sherman, commending her for her teaching and inviting her to return to the school and resume her classes. The district offered her protection from security guards and even an escort from her car to the school door.

For Sherman, it came too late. She wanted to return, but the memory of that awful day in November made it impossible for her. "I just wanted to crawl into a hole because I was afraid," she said. "I can't live like this, day by day. I can't have people at my door or people escorting me from my car to the school because that just totally depreciates the whole idea I was trying to teach my kids about getting along and loving one another."

Sherman wasn't giving up on teaching, but she would not return to P.S. 75. Her request for a transfer was approved on December 2 and she began teaching at P.S. 131 in Queens, New York, the following week. Children and parents at this multiethnic elementary school welcomed Sherman with open arms. "I saw the book and I didn't think it would be a problem at all," said one parent with a fifth grader at P.S. 131. "Nappy hair is part of the black culture, and if you have nappy hair, there is nothing wrong with it. I think her motive was good."

Among Sherman's other defenders was author Carolivia Herron. "[Sherman] could have taught 'Mary Had a Little Lamb' or some other books that had nothing to do with the African-American culture," Herron said. "Instead, she tried to relate to the culture of the children she was teaching."

Eventually teacher and author met and became friends. They have appeared together on television talk shows and at educational conferences to discuss the book and the responses to it. Sherman was even invited back to P.S. 75 to talk to her former students about the experience. But, according to Sherman, the invitation was later withdrawn. "I always thought that I would get to talk to those children," she said with regret.

Further Reading

Carolivia Herron official Web site. Available online: www.carolivia.org. Accessed October 9. 2007.

Foerstel, Herbert N. *Banned in the U.S.A.: A Reference Guide to Book Censorship in Schools and Public Libraries*. Westport, Conn.: Greenwood Press. 2002.

Lyden, Liz. "New York Teacher Runs Into a Racial Divide." *Washington Post*, December 3, 1998: A3.

About the Author of *Nappy Hair*

Carolivia Herron (1947–)

Carolivia Herron is a multitalented author and teacher whose work ranges from Jewish-African studies to children's books. She was born on July 22, 1947, in Washington, D.C. She earned a B.A. degree from Eastern Baptist College in St. Davids, Pennsylvania, and an M.A. in English from Villanova University in 1973. Herron later earned her Ph.D. in comparative literature and literary theory from the University of Pennsylvania. She converted to Judaism as an adult and traces her Jewish roots to her grandmother, a descendant of the Jewish Geechees who lived on Sea Island, Georgia.

Her first novel for adults, *Thereafter Johnnie* (1991), is a semi-autobiographical story of several generations of an African-American family living in Washington. That same year she edited the papers of Angelina Weld Grimké, the celebrated African-American journalist and poet, published by Oxford University Press. Ten years after she wrote *Nappy Hair*, Herron published her second children's book, *Always an Olivia* (2007), about the journey of her ancestors from Tripoli, Libya, to Georgia's Sea Island. She is currently working on a multimedia novel, *Asenath and Our Song of Songs*. On her Web site, Herron describes the book as "an elaborate comic novel, celebrating African and Judaic sources of epic song."

Herron has taught literature at a number of colleges and universities, including Harvard University, Mount Holyoke College, and Brandeis University.

The Perks of Being a Wallflower (1999)
by Stephen Chbosky

What Happens in *The Perks of Being a Wallflower*

Stephen Chbosky's novel is written as a series of letters from the protagonist, Charlie, to an unnamed friend. Charlie is a withdrawn, introverted freshman at a high school in western Pennsylvania. He manages to navigate life by remaining a passive onlooker in a school environment where drugs, sex, and alcohol are being used and abused all around him. He is befriended by two seniors, Patrick and his stepsister Samantha. He soon learns that Patrick is gay and has a crush on Brad, the football team's star quarterback, who is also secretly gay.

Charlie has a few secrets of his own. His best friend, Michael, recently committed suicide. He also feels guilt over the death of his favorite aunt, who died on Christmas Eve in a car accident while driving to buy him a birthday present. Charlie's older sister is being physically abused by a boyfriend, and Charlie gets his first kiss from Samantha, with whom he is hopelessly in love.

With the help of Samantha and Patrick and Bill, an English teacher who takes a personal interest in Charlie, the young man learns how to not just watch life from the sidelines but to become an active participant, hurtful as it sometimes may be.

Challenges and Censorship

Stephen Chbosky claims he was inspired to write his novel by J. D. Salinger's *The Catcher in the Rye*. Like Salinger's protagonist, Holden Caulfield, Chbosky's Charlie is confused and alienated by the world around him. Since its publication by MTV Books in 1999, *The Perks of Being a Wallflower* has become a cult favorite of young readers across the country. As of 2007, some half a million copies of the novel have sold.

Teens have related to the difficulties faced by Charlie and his friends and fellow students. However, the graphic descriptions of alcohol and drug use, as well as sexual relationships and references to suicide, have led to the book being banned in at least two school districts in Massachusetts and Long Island, New York. Many other challenges to the book have been reported. *The Perks of Being a Wallflower* ranked eighth on the American Library Association's "10 Most Frequently Challenged books of 2006."

"When people challenge [my novel], they don't put the offensive scenes in context," said the author in a recent interview. "They say there are drugs and sex in the book, but—while it's not anti-drug or anti-sex—it's certainly not glorified. But it seems like these censors believe that if kids read about it in any context—they're going to engage in it."

On the more positive side, Chbosky claims that he had person-ally heard of two teenagers—a 14-year-old girl and a 17-year-old boy—who didn't commit suicide because they read the book. "I didn't write it to be challenged," he insists. "I didn't write it to be a controversial book. I can't really take it as a point of pride because it was banned someplace."

Landmark Challenge:
"An Issue of Choice" in Arrowhead

"We were shocked and appalled," said Karen Krueger of Arrowhead, Wisconsin, after she and her husband, Kurt, took a good look at the novel that their son, a sophomore at Arrowhead High School, was reading for his modern literature class. The Kruegers decided they "had to do something" about *The Perks of Being a Wallflower*. In late 2004, the couple filed a formal written complaint with the local school board, urging that the novel be removed for profanity and references to sex and rape and suicide.

In December, the school board, along with an ad hoc commit-tee, decided to keep the book in the curriculum, pointing out at the same time that reading it was entirely optional, and that parents could choose to have their children in the class read another book. "If a parent wants to make that decision, we don't have a problem with it," said Christopher Ahmuty, executive director of the American Civil Liberties Union (ACLU) of Wisconsin. "But that decision becomes problematic when it relates to other students such as in a library or classroom."

Karen Krueger saw the issue very differently. "The Constitution applies to taxpaying adults. And as taxpaying adults—as parents—we are responsible for our minor children," she insisted. " . . . To me, it is more an issue of choice, which is not censorship. Choice means choosing one text over another. I think there are better choices and better books out there for students to be reading. Keep the book in the library but take it out of the classroom."

In an unusual move, author Stephen Chbosky wrote a personal letter to the school board, urging them not to give in to pressure from the Kruegers and their supporters. "It's not that I begrudge anybody his or her religious or moral beliefs, but at the same time, it just felt terribly unfair," he explained, discussing the letter in an interview. "This was just one family—and a few families joined their cause to have the book banned—but so many kids in the school district responded to the book, and so many teachers and educators saw the value of the book. . . . I didn't understand why a handful of people could deny it to the whole student body."

The school board's justification for using the book in class, despite its controversial passages, was to generate discussion on important issues and let it act as a "gateway to other, more difficult, literature." But the Kruegers and their supporters felt that the school board was ignoring their concerns. "Look at our voting records, look at our community's standards," Karen Krueger said. "We are not alone in our concern."

When it became apparent that the board would not reverse its decision, Krueger grew more adamant. "Now I want it banned," she told a local newspaper. "Their parental notification is ineffectual."

Landmark Challenge:
The Paragraph That Condemned a Book

It was only one paragraph of *The Perks of Being a Wallflower*, but it convinced one school official to ban the novel from all high school and middle school libraries in Tucson Unified School District (TUSD) in Tucson, Arizona.

In fall 2005 Tom Horne, superintendent of public instruction, received a complaint about the book from a grandmother in Apache Junction. The complaint referred him to a single paragraph that described a boy forcing a girl to perform oral sex at a party. After reading it, Horne was ready to take action. "The page is not just oral sex," he said. "It's nonconsensual oral sex that's described in detail. There's nothing in *Catcher in the Rye* that's remotely comparable to this."

Horne was so disturbed by the passage that he dashed off a letter to regional school principals and superintendents requesting them to examine their policies about the selection of library books. The one book uppermost in his mind was *The Perks*. "I'm hoping that if they have this book on the shelves they make sure that this is no longer available to minors or any other students for that matter and they will check to see if there are any other books like that on their shelves," he said. "I wouldn't dream of trying to stop adults from reading it, but schools should not make this book available to students in their charge."

The superintendent's insistence that he was not instituting censorship was met with skepticism from other officials. "[TUSD] is not in the habit of censorship," said Harriet Scarborough, senior academic officer for curriculum instruction and professional learning. "Once we start taking books off the shelves, we might end up with no books at all."

While admitting that she hadn't read the entire novel, Scarborough questioned Horne's basis for the banning on one paragraph or page. "Just taking a page out of context is not going to make your complaint very valid," she declared. "TUSD leadership will have to do some research and discuss whether removing books like that is something that we want to start practicing." She also saw it as leading to more banning of books. "What is he going to do, check every book in the library and determine if a book has pages like those?" she asked. "We're going to be burning books again. We need to approach something like this with a focus and we need to have a system. We can't be reactionary."

Further Reading

"Arrowhead, Wisconsin." *Newsletter on Intellectual Freedom*, May 2005. Available online: https://members.ala.org/nif/v54n3/dateline.html. Accessed November 21, 2007.

Beckerman, Marty. "An Interview with Stephen Chbosky." Word Riot Web site. Available online: www.wordriot.org/template.php?ID=552. Accessed November 17, 2007.

"Tucson, Arizona." *Newsletter on Intellectual Freedom*, January 2006. Available online: https://members.ala.org/nif/v55n1/dateline.html. Accessed November 21, 2007.

About the Author of *The Perks of Being a Wallflower*

Stephen Chbosky (1970–)

An author, editor, screenwriter, and film director, Stephen Chbosky may have found his greatest success on television as cocreator, executive producer, and writer of the CBS series *Jericho* (2006–).

He was born on January 25, 1970, in Pittsburgh, Pennsylvania, and graduated from the University of Southern California's Filmic Writing Program. He wrote and directed his first film, *The Four Corners of Nowhere* (1995), a satirical story of a hitchhiker who befriends a burnt-out performance artist in Ann Arbor, Michigan. The movie was nominated for the Grand Jury Prize at the Sundance Film Festival and won Narrative Feature honors at the Chicago Underground Film Festival.

After publishing *The Perks of Being a Wallflower* in 1999, Chbosky edited the short-story anthology *Pieces* (2000). In 2001, he appeared on Broadway in the solo comedy *Sexaholic* and wrote the screenplay for the film adaptation of the Broadway musical *Rent* (2005). He was the recipient of the Abraham Polonsky Screenwriting Award for his screenplay *Entirely Divided*. The television series *Jericho*, which debuted on CBS in the fall of 2006, is about life in a small Kansas town after a series of terrorist attacks.

Whale Talk (2001)
by Chris Crutcher

• • • • • • • • • • • • •

What Happens in *Whale Talk*

T. J. Jones has faced many challenges in his young life as an adopted child of black, white, and Japanese heritage. Now he may face the biggest challenge of all—forming a swim team for Cutter High School to help out a favorite teacher, Mr. Simet, who will be the team's coach. Putting the team together gives T. J. a chance to show that the school's losers and misfits can achieve as much, if not more, than proud and bullying jocks like football star Mike Barbour.

T. J. has a personal vendetta against Barbour after he gives Chris Coughlin, who is mentally challenged, a hard time for wearing his dead brother's letter jacket to school, supposedly an infraction of school policy. T. J. recruits Chris for the swim team, along with other misfits who, like T. J., have never participated in school athletics before. They include Dan Hole, a scholarly nerd with an advanced vocabulary; Jackie Craig, a loser who doesn't talk; and hotheaded Andy Mott, who doesn't let having one leg stop him from swimming. T. J. works hard with his teammates—and while they win no swim meets, they do begin to accrue valuable points for the school that could help it win the annual All-Sport trophy. Coach Simet and T. J. make a deal with the Athletic Council, headed by Head Coach Benson, that if each swimmer can best his record with each meet, they will all earn letters.

In a critical subplot, T. J. and his parents take in a mother and her black child, Heidi, who is the stepchild of an abusive former Cutter football hero, Rich Marshall. T. J.'s dad is particularly sensitive to

Heidi's needs. Years earlier, he had accidentally killed a young child, running over it with his truck. Tension builds as the swim team's season draws near its end and Marshall threatens the Jones family to get his child and her mother back.

T. J. ends up deliberately losing a race at the state finals when he learns that the Athletic Council, behind the team's back, has voted to refuse them their letters. In the end, ironically, every team member does get his letter, except for T. J., the best swimmer, who did not improve his record in his last race.

This happy ending is marred by tragedy, when a half-insane Marshall tries to shoot Heidi with a hunting rifle. T. J.'s father rushes in and takes the bullet instead. As he lies dying, Mr. Jones makes his son swear not to seek revenge for his death. Marshall goes to prison for life, Mike Barbour finally changes his ways and becomes a better person, and T. J. and his mother take Heidi, her mother, and her siblings into their home permanently.

Challenges and Censorship

On its publication in 2001, *Whale Talk* was received with glowing reviews. *Publishers Weekly* called it a "gripping tale of small-town prejudice [that] delivers a frank, powerful message about social issues and ills."

Crutcher's abrasive depiction of these prejudices and the frank language he used led to frequent challenges in schools. In January 2005 the superintendent of the South Carolina State Board of Education removed the book from the suggested reading list of a pilot English-literature curriculum. A month later, it was attacked by challenges at Grand Ledge High School in Michigan. *Whale Talk* was ranked fifth on the American Library Association's "10 Most Frequently Challenged Books of 2005" for "racism and offensive language."

Crutcher himself, in a letter to the school board in the landmark challenge below, singled out what he believed was the most offensive passage in the novel, in which Heidi, a four-year-old girl of mixed race, spews out the racism her stepfather has subjected her to in a play therapy session. "In the course of her therapy," Crutcher wrote, "she is taking the role of the offender, yelling out all the names that she herself endures on a daily basis. Because she is screaming the words, they are in large font, which, I assume, makes them even more offensive to those paging through the book. The scene read in the context of the story, I believe, is heartbreaking. It is also true. It is something I have seen played out by a real four and a half year old mixed race girl in that very situation."

Landmark Challenge:
An Author Challenges the Challengers

While authors sometimes follow challenges to books they've written, it's not often that an author gets directly involved in the challenge. But then Chris Crutcher is not your everyday young-adult author. He feels passionately about censorship and he's not afraid to speak out about it.

In November 2004, Crutcher's novel *Whale Talk* was challenged by Christi Brooks, a parent of a student at Ardmore High School in Decatur, Alabama. While admitting that the book "is talking about teamwork and dealing with racism," Brooks felt that students who read it "would be more likely to use the [bad] words every day."

Ardmore senior and school library aide Sheila Foster strongly disagreed. "I was brought up that I wouldn't get away with saying things like that," she told members of the Limestone County Board of Education. "Kids can probably hear worse language riding on the school bus. Some books have pretty good points. You just have to get past the language. I know the board members need to protect themselves because people file lawsuits for anything these days. But to me, it definitely would be hard to say, 'Don't let every person read this book.' Everyone is different."

The school board handed the matter over to a review committee composed of staff members and parents. The committee recommended that the board retain *Whale Talk* in all county high school libraries, claiming that "The message of the book is more important than the language used." The recommendation was fully supported by school superintendent Barry Carroll. But the school board saw it otherwise.

In a 4 to 3 vote on March 7, 2005, the board moved to ban the book from all school libraries. The book's profanity was the deciding factor in its decision. "We can't allow students to go down our halls and say those words, and we shouldn't let them read it," said board member James Shannon. "That book's got a lot of bad, bad words."

Author Crutcher followed the case closely and wrote an online open letter to the people of Limestone County, especially the school board. "Stories like *Whale Talk* . . . let them [students] know they are not alone, while not forcing them to talk about their personal situation at the same time," he wrote. "When we censor these stories, we censor the kids themselves. Imagine falling in love with a book because somehow it mirrors your life, and gives meaning to it, and may even offer solutions to your personal situation, only to have those in power over you censor it because it is offensive. All but the most hard nosed of us might think our very lives were offensive."

In a second letter, written to the students of Limestone County themselves, Crutcher was less circumspect. "I think it is obscene that your school board does not trust you enough to know you can read harsh stories, told in their native tongue, and make decisions for yourself what you think of the issues or the language."

Neither Crutcher nor other local defenders of the book swayed the board to change its decision. However, at the board's May meeting, an impassioned Creekside librarian, Janet Saczawa, spoke for the county's school librarians and issued her own challenge. "It is obvious to many of us that some of the board members have not read the book in its entirety," said Saczawa. "In doing so, you have violated your own board policy, which states that you will read the material being challenged in its entirety, not just Xeroxed copies of the offending passages. . . . Some of our students face similar situations [to the characters in the book] every day. You do these students a disservice if you remove this book and others like it from our schools, thereby telling them that you are offended by their stories, their situations, their pain, and ultimately, by them."

The ban stood, but author Crutcher may have had the last word. He donated five copies of *Whale Talk* to the Athens-Limestone Public Library. Perhaps he felt if students couldn't read his novel in their school library, they could at least access a copy at the public library. "The kids you turn your backs on when you take away their stories are the ones who lose, as well as you as a community of adults who may appear to fear their truths," Crutcher wrote the board in his letter. "Remember, if you take *Whale Talk* out, you can take any book out."

Further Reading

Crutcher, Chris. "In Response to the *Whale Talk* Challenge in Alabama." Chris Crutcher official Web site. Available online: www.abffe. org/bbw-crutcher.htm. Accessed November 7, 2007.

"Decatur, Alabama." *Newsletter on Intellectual Freedom*, July 2005. Available online: https://members.ala.org/nif/v54n4/dateline.html. Accessed November 21, 2007.

"Joint Letter to Missouri Valley High School Superintendent about Removing *Whale Talk* from High School Curriculum," March 7, 2007. National Coalition Against Censorship Web site. Available online: www.ncac.org/literature/20070307~IA-Missouri_Valley~Joint_ Letter_To_Missouri_Valley_Superintendent_About_Whale_Talk. cfm. Accessed November 7, 2007.

"Limestone County, Alabama." *Newsletter on Intellectual Freedom*, May 2005. Available online: https://members.ala.org/nif/v54n3/dateline. html. Accessed November 21, 2007.

About the Author of *Whale Talk*

Chris Crutcher (1946–   )

Chris Crutcher was born on July 17, 1946, in Dayton, Ohio. His father was an Air Force pilot and his mother a homemaker. Later, the family moved to Cascade, Idaho, a small logging town north of Boise, the state capital. He attended Eastern Washington State College and earned a degree in sociology and psychology. Crutcher was a swimmer and distance runner in college, and sports play a major role in much of his fiction.

Crutcher taught at a California alternative school before moving to Spokane, Washington, where he works as a child and family therapist. His first young-adult novel, *Running Loose*, was published in 1983 and was named an American Library Association (ALA) Best Book for Young Adult Readers. His next three novels—*Stotan!* (1986), *The Crazy Horse Electric Game* (1987), and *Chinese Handcuffs* (1989)—were similarly honored, as was *Athletic Shorts* (1991), a collection of short stories.

In 1998 Crutcher received the Intellectual Freedom Award from the National Council of Teachers of English. He was also the recipient of the Margaret A. Edwards Award in 2000 for excellence in young-adult literature. Some of his most recent novels include *Whale Talk* (2001), *The Sledding Hill* (2005), and *Deadline* (2007). His fascinating "ill-advised" autobiography, *King of the Mild Frontier*, was published in 2003.

"I won't back off on a story because I think someone will be offended by it," Crutcher has said. "I may be judicious in what I should write about; but once I decide, I won't leave anything out."

America (2002)
by E. R. Frank

What Happens in *America*

America is a 15-year-old biracial youth whose life has been one trauma after another. Born to a crack addict, America is adopted by a rich white family. However, when his skin darkens by age five, they want nothing more to do with him. The caring nanny of the family, Sylvia Harper, adopts America, but after a year the state sends him back to live with his biological mother and two older half brothers in New York City.

Following the bad example of his brothers, America engages in petty crimes, including theft and vandalism. When the three are caught committing a crime, America is sent to a hospital and eventually returns to live with Mrs. Harper. While she is at work, Mrs. Harper leaves America in the care of her half brother Browning, who begins to molest the eight-year-old. Depressed by and angry at this abuse, the boy sets fire to Browning's bed, killing him. He flees to New York City and lives for a time with a drug dealer named Ty. He is soon picked up by the police and confesses to Browning's murder, but due to his young age he cannot be convicted of the crime.

A judge sends America to Applegate, a mental hospital. Despairing that he will never live a normal life, he tries to commit suicide by hanging himself with shoelaces. His attempt fails and he is sent to Ridgeway Hospital in New York, where he is befriended by Dr. B, a psychiatrist. Under Dr. B's care, America begins to open up and tell his story. Dr. B offers him hope and helps him get into a transitional home where America, now 17, will live with two other young men and a social worker. America visits Mrs. Harper in a nursing home, days before she dies. In a dream, the young man envisions a new life in which God uplifts him. The terrible nightmare is finally over.

Challenges and Censorship

While it hasn't made any ALA "10 Most Frequently Challenged Books" lists since its publication in 2002, *America* has still faced its share of challenges for language and sexual situations. Author E. R. Frank wrote the book about one abused boy, but now says the character represents many thousands of abused children. "[A]fter it was completed, it became clear that the part of me who is outraged by how children are treated in our child-welfare and criminal justice systems and by how we continue to neglect assisting and educating adults who need help parenting, was slyly at work in the writing of that book as well."

Like many other banned authors, Frank sees very little as being off-limits for serious writers for young adults. "My feeling about literature and art and this country is that we can all say whatever we want in whatever we want to, as long as our expressions are not, in and of themselves, a tool with which to carry out imminent physical harm to others," she has said. While Frank has no problem with representative groups of teachers and parents removing a book of hers from a school library after serious deliberation, she has a big problem with those who don't know what they're doing. "If . . . a few people in that county have read bits of [my book] and, without formal process and discussion with the community, yank it off the high school shelves, I find that to be reactionary, insulting, and a shame. Even if the latter scenario is the case, I wouldn't lose sleep over it. That's just not the kind of the thing I stew over."

America has been optioned for a film by actress and talk-show host Rosie O'Donnell, who had Frank as a guest on her talk show soon after the novel's publication.

Landmark Challenge:
No Pretty Picture in Twin Bridges, Montana

Teachers are usually defending books, not challenging them, but such was not the case in Twin Bridges, Montana, in early 2004. "I believe a school library has a higher calling than public libraries to provide appropriate materials for students," said Twin Bridges teacher Mark Weber, in his request to remove *America* from district school libraries. His complaint was based on inappropriate language and graphic sexual imagery. "This is about kids and what's best for them," Weber added, requesting that the school board set up a committee that would reflect "local values" in the selection of reading texts.

Instead, the school board appointed a committee to evaluate the novel and Weber's challenge. The committee made its recommendation to keep the novel, claiming that the book was a valid and realistic picture of an abused child and his experiences. "Abuse cannot be painted with a pretty picture," reported the committee.

At a June meeting of the school board, which 80 people attended, others felt differently. To point out the book's inappropriateness, Jamie Mehlhoff began to read aloud passages that she considered, in the parlance of movie ratings, X-rated. Board members asked her not to continue. When she did anyway, they adjourned the meeting. This did not sit well with those who supported the challenge. "If you can't read a book out loud, it doesn't belong in the school library," reasoned Krista Berry.

But many others opposed the banning of *America*. "I am my children's censor," declared Karen Degel. "I am not your child's censor. I take an active role in what my kids read."

"If this book is removed, Pandora's box will be opened," said Twin Bridges school librarian Jamie Reynolds. "Though one group of people so adamantly objects to profanity, there are other groups who feel just as strongly about religion, fantasy or witchcraft, gay rights, evolution, and the list goes on."

The board apparently agreed with this assessment. In closed session that same evening, members voted 4 to 1 to follow the committee's recommendation and keep *America* in their school libraries.

Landmark Challenge: "Not Suitable for Any Child"

America is not on any reading list at Brown Middle School in Ravenna, Ohio, but that didn't stop Angela Calo, the mother of a seventh grader, from seeking its withdrawal from the district. The novel was included in a free reading library in a gifted and talented class at Brown taught by Cathy Adler. Adler warned students before they read the novel that it contained "raw material." Too raw for middle school students, according to Calo's complaint.

"The book has inappropriate language and sexual activities, such as masturbation, that is for adult content only," Calo said. "What we kept finding and going over was sexual content and profanity. Yes, we decided it was not suitable for any child."

After receiving Calo's written complaint, superintendent of schools Tim Calfee had committee members read and review the book's content, as called for by district policy. "The reviews are actually pretty positive," Calfee said. "The book deals with problems that unfortunately are all too common in our society, but they are types of things you hear about on the news everyday."

Based on the letters that appeared in the local newspaper, the *Ravenna Record-Courier*, most parents agreed with him. "Mrs. Calo certainly has the right to make decisions for her family, but she does not get to decide for my family, or yours," wrote one parent with a child in the same gifted class taught by Mrs. Adler. "This is about book banning. It is not about how good a teacher is. Anyone who knows Cathy Adler has no question about that. *America* is not a book teaching the birds and bees. It is about a troubled child and the horrible things he goes through in 'the system' throughout the years. It might be about a child you know."

As the review committee went about its work, Calo was looking forward to more challenges. She planned to go after two books scheduled to be placed on the 2007–08 approved reading list—Laurie Halse Anderson's *Speak* and Chris Crutcher's *Staying Fat for Sarah Byrnes*. Author E. R. Frank responded to the challenge in Ravenna by declaring, "Books shouldn't be censored by the distress of one parent. I am honored to be in the same company as authors Anderson and Crutcher."

Further Reading

Atkins, Holly. "An Interview with E. R. Frank." *St. Petersburg Times*, February 16, 2004. Available online: www.sptimes.com/2004/02/16/ Nie/An_Interview_with_ER_.shtml. Accessed October 29, 2007.

DeLeon, Jason. "Mom Seeks to Ban Book in Ravenna; Parent Says Material Too Adult for Students." *Ravenna Record-Courier*, March 14, 2007. Available online: www.recordpub.com/news/article/1720011. Accessed November 13, 2007.

"An Interview with E. R. Frank." Embracing the Child Web site. Available online: www.embracingthechild.org/afrank.html. Accessed November 2, 2007.

"Ravenna, Ohio." *Newsletter on Intellectual Freedom*, May 2007. Available online: https://members.ala.org/nif/v56n3/dateline.html. Accessed November 21, 2007.

"School Board Votes to Keep Book on Library Shelves." First Amendment Center Web site, June 16, 2004. Available online: www.firstamend mentcenter.org/news.aspx?id=13531. Accessed November 13, 2007.

About the Author of *America*

E. R. Frank (1968–   )

E. R. Frank is on the cutting edge of young-adult fiction, writing about young people at extremes in American society. She was born Emily Frank in 1968. Prior to turning to writing, she was a clinical social worker and later a psychotherapist specializing in trauma.

Frank's first novel, *Life Is Funny* (2000), is the story of 11 young people and their problems over a seven-year period. The book was winner of the Teen People Book Club NEXT Award for Young Adult Fiction. *America* (2002) was her second novel. Her most recent work, *Wrecked* (2006), is about a teen girl who is responsible for the death of her brother's girlfriend in a car accident.

Frank continues to work as a psychotherapist in New York City. Although her patients often inspire her writing, she has consciously not written about real people in her books. "These characters are the result of my cumulative experiences and imaginings," she said in one interview. "They could easily have walked through my office doors, but instead they have settled in my heart."

APPENDIX 1

The American Library Association's "100 Most Frequently Challenged Books of 1990–2000"

(Books and authors in **boldface** are included in the **Our Freedom to Read** series.)

1. *Scary Stories* **series, by Alvin Schwartz**
2. *Daddy's Roommate,* by Michael Willhoite
3. *I Know Why the Caged Bird Sings,* by Maya Angelou
4. *The Chocolate War,* **by Robert Cormier**
5. *The Adventures of Huckleberry Finn,* **by Mark Twain**
6. *Of Mice and Men,* **by John Steinbeck**
7. *Harry Potter* **series, by J. K. Rowling**
8. *Forever,* **by Judy Blume**
9. *Bridge to Terabithia,* by Katherine Paterson
10. *Alice* **series, by Phyllis Reynolds Naylor**
11. *Heather Has Two Mommies,* by Leslea Newman
12. *My Brother Sam Is Dead,* **by James Lincoln Collier and Christopher Collier**
13. *The Catcher in the Rye,* **by J. D. Salinger**
14. *The Giver,* **by Lois Lowry**
15. *It's Perfectly Normal,* by Robie Harris
16. *Goosebumps* **series, by R. L. Stine**
17. *A Day No Pigs Would Die,* by Robert Newton Peck
18. *The Color Purple,* by Alice Walker
19. *Sex,* by Madonna
20. *Earth's Children* series, by Jean M. Auel

21. *The Great Gilly Hopkins,* **by Katherine Paterson**
22. *A Wrinkle in Time,* **by Madeleine L'Engle**
23. *Go Ask Alice,* **by Anonymous**
24. *Fallen Angels,* **by Walter Dean Myers**
25. *In the Night Kitchen,* **by Maurice Sendak**
26. *The Stupids* **series, by Harry Allard**
27. *The Witches,* **by Roald Dahl**
28. *The New Joy of Gay Sex,* by Charles Silverstein
29. *Anastasia Krupnik* series, by Lois Lowry
30. *The Goats,* **by Brock Cole**
31. *Kaffir Boy,* by Mark Mathabane
32. *Blubber,* **by Judy Blume**
33. *Killing Mr. Griffin,* **by Lois Duncan**
34. *Halloween ABC,* **by Eve Merriam**
35. *We All Fall Down,* **by Robert Cormier**
36. *Final Exit,* by Derek Humphry
37. *The Handmaid's Tale,* by Margaret Atwood
38. *Julie of the Wolves,* **by Jean Craighead George**
39. *The Bluest Eye,* **by Toni Morrison**
40. *What's Happening to My Body? Book for Girls,* by Lynda Madaras
41. *To Kill a Mockingbird,* **by Harper Lee**
42. *Beloved,* by Toni Morrison
43. *The Outsiders,* **by S. E. Hinton**
44. *The Pigman,* **by Paul Zindel**
45. *Bumps in the Night,* by Harry Allard
46. *Deenie,* **by Judy Blume**
47. *Flowers for Algernon,* by Daniel Keyes
48. *Annie on My Mind,* **by Nancy Garden**
49. *The Boy Who Lost His Face,* by Louis Sachar
50. *Cross Your Fingers, Spit in Your Hat,* by Alvin Schwartz
51. *A Light in the Attic,* **by Shel Silverstein**
52. *Brave New World,* **by Aldous Huxley**
53. *Sleeping Beauty Trilogy,* by A. N. Roquelaure (Anne Rice)
54. *Asking About Sex and Growing Up,* by Joanna Cole
55. *Cujo,* **by Stephen King**
56. *James and the Giant Peach,* **by Roald Dahl**
57. *The Anarchist Cookbook,* by William Powell
58. *Boys and Sex,* by Wardell Pomeroy

59. *Ordinary People,* by Judith Guest
60. *American Psycho,* by Bret Easton Ellis
61. *What's Happening to My Body? Book for Boys,* by Lynda Madaras
62. *Are You There God? It's Me, Margaret,* by Judy Blume
63. *Crazy Lady,* by Jane Conly
64. **Athletic Shorts, by Chris Crutcher**
65. *Fade,* by Robert Cormier
66. *Guess What?,* by Mem Fox
67. *The House of Spirits,* by Isabel Allende
68. *The Face on the Milk Carton,* by Caroline Cooney
69. *Slaughterhouse-Five,* by Kurt Vonnegut
70. *Lord of the Flies,* by William Golding
71. *Native Son,* by Richard Wright
72. *Women on Top: How Real Life Has Changed Women's Sexual Fantasies,* by Nancy Friday
73. **Curses, Hexes & Spells, by Daniel Cohen**
74. **Jack, by A.M. Homes**
75. *Bless Me, Ultima,* by Rudolfo A. Anaya
76. *Where Did I Come From?,* by Peter Mayle
77. *Carrie,* by Stephen King
78. *Tiger Eyes,* by Judy Blume
79. *On My Honor,* by Marion Dane Bauer
80. *Arizona Kid,* by Ron Koertge
81. *Family Secrets,* by Norma Klein
82. *Mommy Laid an Egg,* by Babette Cole
83. *The Dead Zone,* by Stephen King
84. **The Adventures of Tom Sawyer, by Mark Twain**
85. *Song of Solomon,* by Toni Morrison
86. *Always Running,* by Luis Rodriguez
87. *Private Parts,* by Howard Stern
88. *Where's Waldo?,* by Martin Hanford
89. **Summer of My German Soldier, by Bette Greene**
90. **Little Black Sambo, by Helen Bannerman**
91. *Pillars of the Earth,* by Ken Follett
92. *Running Loose,* by Chris Crutcher
93. *Sex Education,* by Jenny Davis
94. **The Drowning of Stephan Jones, by Bette Greene**
95. *Girls and Sex,* by Wardell Pomeroy

96. *How to Eat Fried Worms,* by Thomas Rockwell
97. *View from the Cherry Tree,* by Willo Davis Roberts
98. *The Headless Cupid,* by Zilpha Keatley Snyder
99. *The Terrorist,* by Caroline Cooney
100. *Jump Ship to Freedom,* by James Lincoln Collier and Christopher Collier

APPENDIX 2

The American Library Association's "10 Most Frequently Challenged Books of 2006" and the Reasons for the Challenges

(Books and authors in **boldface** are included in the **Our Freedom to Read** series.)

1. *And Tango Makes Three,* by Justin Richardson and Peter Parnell, for homosexuality, antifamily content, and being unsuited to age group
2. *Gossip Girls* series, by Cecily Von Ziegesar, for homosexuality, sexual content, drugs, being unsuited to age group, and offensive language
3. ***Alice* series, by Phyllis Reynolds Naylor,** for sexual content and offensive language
4. ***The Earth, My Butt, and Other Big Round Things,* by Carolyn Mackler,** for sexual content, antifamily content, offensive language, and being unsuited to age group
5. ***The Bluest Eye,* by Toni Morrison,** for sexual content, offensive language, and being unsuited to age group
6. ***Scary Stories* series, by Alvin Schwartz,** for occultism/Satanism, being unsuited to age group, violence, and insensitivity
7. ***Athletic Shorts,* by Chris Crutcher,** for homosexuality and offensive language
8. ***The Perks of Being a Wallflower,* by Stephen Chbosky,** for homosexuality, sexual content, offensive language, and being unsuited to age group

9. *Beloved,* by Toni Morrison, for offensive language, sexual content, and being unsuited to age group

10. *The Chocolate War,* by **Robert Cormier,** for sexual content, offensive language, and violence

APPENDIX 3

The American Library Association's "10 Most Frequently Challenged Books of 2007" and the Reasons for the Challenges

(Books and authors in **boldface** are included in the **Our Freedom to Read** series.)

1. *And Tango Makes Three,* by Justin Richardson and Peter Parnell, for anti-ethnic content, sexism, homosexuality, antifamily content, its religious viewpoint, and being unsuited to age group
2. *The Chocolate War,* **by Robert Cormier,** for sexual content, offensive language, and violence
3. *Olive's Ocean,* by Kevin Henkes, for sexual content and offensive language
4. *The Golden Compass,* **by Philip Pullman,** for its religious viewpoint
5. *The Adventures of Huckleberry Finn,* **by Mark Twain,** for racism
6. *The Color Purple,* by Alice Walker, for homosexuality, sexual content, offensive language, and being unsuited to age group
7. *TTYL,* by Lauren Myracle, for sexual content, offensive language, and being unsuited to age group
8. *I Know Why the Caged Bird Sings,* by Maya Angelou, for sexual content
9. *It's Perfectly Normal,* by Robie Harris, for sexual content
10. *The Perks of Being a Wallflower,* **by Stephen Chbosky,** for homosexuality, sexual content, offensive language, and being unsuited to age group

APPENDIX 4

Web sites on Book Censorship and Challenges

American Booksellers Foundation for Free Expression
www.abffe.org
This site is useful for its Banned Books Week Handbook, which includes many interesting features such as "Stories Behind the Bans and Challenges."

American Library Association
www.ala.org
The official Web site of the ALA has a wealth of information on challenged and banned books, including yearly lists of the top challenged books and archives for the ALA's Newsletter on Intellectual Freedom.

National Coalition Against Censorship
www.ncac.org
This site includes updated news on censorship issues, including Supreme Court decisions. There is information on censorship of not only books, but also art, music, science, and entertainment.

APPENDIX 5

Banned Books Week

Early each fall, the American Library Association (ALA) sponsors Banned Books Week nationwide. It is an opportunity for everyone who loves to read—and cherishes the freedom to do so—to draw attention to that precious right. The first Banned Books Week was celebrated in 1981.

Here are some ways the ALA's Office for Intellectual Freedom suggests you can celebrate Banned Books Week:

1. Read a banned book. Look for a favorite or something you've never read before on the book lists in Appendixes 1, 2, and 3. You might choose one of the books discussed in this volume.
2. Talk about the First Amendment in school. Make it the focus of a class discussion. The First Amendment to the U.S. Constitution reads: "Congress shall make no law respecting an establishment of religion, or prohibiting the free exercise thereof; or abridging the freedom of speech, or of the press; or of the people peaceably to assemble, and to petition the Government for a redress of grievances."
3. Organize your own Banned Books Read-Out! at your school, public library, or a local bookstore. Invite a local author, banned or otherwise, to read from his or her work. Have adults and children read selections from banned books.
4. Join IFAN, the Intellectual Freedom Action Network, a grassroots group of volunteers who are willing to come forward in defense of the freedom to read in censorship controversies in your school or community.

5. Join another organization that advocates intellectual freedom, such as the Freedom to Read Foundation.

6. Write or call your government representatives in Washington, D.C., and let them know you want them to protect your freedom to read in their role as legislators.

If you have your own ideas for how to celebrate Banned Books Week, e-mail them to the Office for Intellectual Freedom at oif@ala.org. They'd be happy to hear from you!

INDEX